SUPERHEROES ON THE SPECTRUM

BY
Rev. Jeannette Paxia and Dr. Crystal Morrison

Illustrations by Patrick Barr and Dakota Winstead

Superheroes on the Spectrum

DEDICATION

Rev. Jeannette Paxia:

This book is dedicated to my son Jacob, I loved you unconditionally from the moment I found out I was pregnant. I dreamed of all the experiences we would have together. Our life has surpassed all of my wildest dreams and although there have been challenges, I wouldn't change any of it. You were my inspiration for this book, and I am grateful for all you have taught me.

To my son Luke, your unique life perspective and talent surprise and delight me daily, I cannot wait to see the mark you will make in this world. To my stepchildren, Bradlee, Ashton, and Samantha, being part of your life has been a bonus and a blessing. I am proud that you all are working towards your dreams. I hope you don't ever lose sight of those.

To my husband, Brian, I could not do all that I do without your continued love and support, adventure continues to await us.

To the contributors we couldn't have done this without your willingness to share, I appreciate each one of you.

To my co-author, Crystal, it has been fun being on this journey with you. I look forward to all we will accomplish together.

Dr. Crystal Morrison:

This book is dedicated to all neurodiverse Superheroes and the Superheroes in their lives.

To my children, you are each remarkable and I'm honored to be your mother. You will always be my "babies" even when you're 63.

To my husband, your unwavering love, support, and partnership are the keys for me to keep traveling this journey.

To our contributors, we are eternally grateful that you've shared your stories and entrusted us to help bring your words to the world.

To my co-author, Jeannette, teamwork makes the dream work and the dream is coming to life in these pages.

To our readers, we see you, we are with you, and we are cheering you on. We give you this book to reject judgment in favor of understanding, acceptance, and celebration. May this book be a beacon of hope and a reminder that our differences are our strengths.

TABLE OF CONTENTS

FOREWORD

by Kevin Mohler

Co-founder of the American Autism and Rehabilitation Center

In the pages of "Superheroes on the Spectrum," you will find a collection of stories that inspire, educate, and illuminate the lives of individuals with special needs. It is a privilege to write this foreword and edify the incredible work of Rev. Jeannette Paxia and Dr. Crystal Morrison, along with the dedicated contributors who have come together to share their experiences, insights, and wisdom.

For the past decade, my mother and I have had the honor of owning the American Autism & Rehabilitation Center, a facility that has touched the lives of tens of thousands of individuals with special needs through countless patient visits each year. Alongside our center, we have also championed the cause of neurodiversity through the American Autism & Rehabilitation Foundation. These endeavors have shown us, time and again, the incredible potential and unique gifts that individuals with special needs bring to the world.

It is essential to remember that children with special needs are not broken; they are special. They are remarkable individuals with talents and abilities that have been bestowed upon them by a higher power. They are, in every sense of the word, superheroes in their own right. Their strength, resilience, and the love they inspire in their families are testaments to their exceptional nature.

As a society, it is our understanding of these individuals that needs to change, not their understanding of the world. When we embrace neuro-diversity and advocate for inclusion, remarkable transformations occur.

The message is clear: when we open our hearts and minds to the incredible diversity of human experience, we unlock the potential for growth, innovation, and compassion that exists within each of us. Children with special needs are precious in the eyes of God, and they should be cherished and celebrated by the rest of the world.

Through "Superheroes on the Spectrum," Rev. Jeannette Paxia and Dr. Crystal Morrison invite us to step into the shoes of these remarkable individuals and their families. They beckon us to join the journey of understanding, acceptance, and appreciation for the beauty of neurodi-versity. This book is a testament to the power of storytelling, the strength of the human spirit, and the limitless potential that resides within every individual, regardless of their unique abilities and challenges.

May the stories within these pages serve as a beacon of hope and inspiration for all who read them.

Kevin Mohler

Vice President
American Autism & Rehabilitation Center
AmericanAutismCenter.com

President
American Autism & Rehabilitation Foundation
AmericanAutismCenter.org

INTRODUCTION
by Rev. Jeannette Paxia

This book was born from a significant event during my son's early years, coupled with my deep desire to increase global understanding of individuals diagnosed on the autism spectrum. It's my hope that we can use these stories to celebrate the unique abilities of people who may be considered different for whatever reason or diagnosis. While autism is the primary focus of this book, this sentiment extends beyond it.

Different is not "bad." No two people are the same and imagine how dull the world would be if we were all identical? This fact was perhaps best stated when Dr. Stephen Shore said, "When you meet one person with Autism, you've met one person with Autism."

When my son Jacob was little, I felt like we had no one to turn to for support. Support groups and social media connections didn't exist then. There is much greater awareness now than there was in those days. We constantly advocated for him, and it was an uphill battle to get a diagnosis and assistance.

I remember when he was in the first grade, and I was at the school once again, because Jacob had disrupted the class. In the meeting with the psychiatrist, he told me that I was wrong about Jacob and that he didn't need additional support in school, he was just acting out. After evaluating him, the psychiatrist apologized to me and said that I had been correct. There were many similar situations where we advocated and pushed the limits to get the support we needed for him. You know your child better than anyone else. Trust yourself, advocate for your child, and know you aren't alone.

Just like my co-author, I also believe it takes a village to raise a child, and I want to make sure to mention some of our villages. Jacob's father, Chris Stolle, has always fought for Jacob. When Jacob was a teenager, I had to accept a job out of state to support us. We would have faced major setbacks if we moved Jacob since he was routine-driven and finally settled in a good school. Going through puberty was also challenging, and Chris cared for him through much of this time. Jacob's grandma, Lynne Ford, has provided unconditional love and support to both of my kids. For Jacob, she was the person who forged the trail for me to learn the importance of advocating. Her youngest son and the boys' uncle, Josh, has severe cerebral palsy, and she has tirelessly advocated for him to make sure he lives life to the fullest. Josh has also been there as an example and loving uncle. Lynne has been more of a 2nd mom to Jacob than a grandma. Both my parents have passed, but my mom, Pat, loved her grandchildren more than anything and did what she could for Jacob. My father, Vito, thoroughly enjoyed conversing with and sharing many similarities with Jacob. Watching them together always touched my heart. My husband, Brian, has connected with Jacob on a level of understanding and as an additional role model. He loves both my children unconditionally and has been a constant support. As a Continuous Improvement Manager, Brian was able to offer Jacob another level of guidance using continuous improvement to work through some of his challenges as a person with neurodiversity. Brian is in turn grateful for every lesson he learned from his many discussions with Jacob. I am amazed at how much all of us learn from Jacob. Last but not least, I want to thank the many teachers and school staff who do a difficult job with little reward. There were many teachers, school specialists, counselors, occupational therapists, and one-on-one aides who were so special to Jacob. They would tell me that Jacob has the biggest heart, and he does. He will do everything he can to support his family, one of his friends, or an animal that is in need.

Three of the teachers/specialists who have been particularly important are Jonathan, Mr. D, and Jacquie. There are many I didn't mention, for all of you who have worked with Jacob, please know I sincerely appreciate all you have done for him.

I also want to mention the controversial puzzle piece symbol, which is the most recognized symbol of autism. I have received some negative comments about using this symbol as part of the cover. Both my co-author and I realize that for some, the puzzle piece is not a symbol they associate with the diagnosis or themselves. I believe that we all are entitled to our opinions. As a speaker, I have always referred to each one of us, with or without a diagnosis, as a piece of a puzzle, and together we make the world go round. We talk more about symbols, terminology and language in the next chapter.

Thank you to all who are reading this book. I truly hope it makes a positive difference in your life.

BOOK PHILOSOPHY
by Dr. Crystal Morrison

- The underlying philosophy behind this book is the awareness, acceptance, and celebration of our neurodiverse experiences.

- While we share the various challenges we have all faced, we also highlight the gifts and new perspectives that neurodiversity has given all of us.

- Just as autism is a spectrum, our contributors are a spectrum of diverse voices including autistic adults, autistic children, parents, and family members of autistic individuals.

- Our contributors live across the United States, the United Kingdom, and South Africa and have vastly different perspectives on symbols, language, causes, and treatment.

- Our contributors include non-speaking autistic adults and children as well as moms and dads.

- The diversity of our contributors and their perspectives is central to our philosophy of awareness, acceptance, and celebration of all things related to autism.

- To honor our contributors, we have preserved the language they use related to diagnosis (such as severity levels, functioning and Asperger's) and identity (person-first vs identity-first). In addition, we have used many of the various symbols that our contributors identify with on our cover including the puzzle piece, color spectrum, and infinity symbol.

- Our effort is not to "make everyone happy." Our effort is to honor the diversity of perspectives today while focusing on awareness, acceptance, and celebration of strengths.

- We've all faced too much judgment and criticism in our lives and there's no place for more of that in these pages.

AUTISM DIAGNOSIS, SYMBOLS, TERMINOLOGY AND USING RESPECTFUL LANGUAGE

by Dr. Crystal Morrison

Diagnosis

The diagnosis of autism is typically based on criteria outlined in the fifth edition of the Diagnostic and Statistical Manual of Mental Disorders (DSM-5) and the International Classification of Diseases (ICD-10 and ICD-11). The DSM-5 is primarily used in the United States and is published by the American Psychiatric Association (APA). Its main purpose is to provide a standardized system for the classification and diagnosis of mental disorders, including mood disorders, anxiety disorders, personality disorders, and neurodevelopmental disorders like autism. The ICD-11 is an international classification system published by the World Health Organization (WHO). It is used globally for a wide range of healthcare and epidemiological purposes, not just mental health. Its primary purpose is to classify diseases and health conditions for statistical and billing purposes, as well as for public health and research.

DSM-5 Criteria:

The DSM-5, published in 2013, introduced changes in the way autism is diagnosed. It uses a single term, "Autism Spectrum Disorder" (ASD), which encompasses a range of symptoms and severity levels. Diagnosis is based on two core domains:

Social Communication and Interaction Impairments:

- Deficits in social-emotional reciprocity (e.g., difficulties in understanding and responding to social cues).
- Deficits in nonverbal communicative behaviors (e.g., limited eye contact, facial expressions, gestures).
- Deficits in developing and maintaining relationships (e.g., challenges with forming friendships).

Restricted, Repetitive Patterns of Behavior, Interests, or Activities:

- Stereotyped or repetitive motor movements, use of objects, or speech (e.g., hand-flapping, echolalia).
- Insistence on sameness or inflexible adherence to routines (e.g., becoming upset with minor changes).
- Highly restricted, fixated interests that are abnormal in intensity or focus.
- Hyper- or hypo-reactivity to sensory input (e.g., heightened sensitivity to certain sounds or textures).

To receive an ASD diagnosis, an individual must display symptoms in both core domains and meet specific criteria within each domain.

ICD-11 Criteria:

The ICD-11, which was released in 2018, also includes a diagnostic category for Autism Spectrum Disorder (ASD). The ICD-11 criteria share similarities with the DSM-5 criteria, focusing on social communication impairments and restricted, repetitive behaviors and interests.

Multidisciplinary Assessment:

- Diagnosis typically involves a comprehensive evaluation by a multidisciplinary team, including clinical psychologists, pediatricians, psychiatrists, speech-language pathologists, and other specialists.
- Assessment tools, observation, and interviews with parents or caregivers are commonly used to gather information about an individual's behavior and developmental history.

Severity Levels:

- Both the DSM-5 and ICD-11 recognize different levels of severity within the autism spectrum, ranging from mild to severe.
- These levels are used to describe the extent of support an individual may need in various areas of life, including social interactions, communication, and daily living skills.

It's important to note that the criteria and guidelines for diagnosing autism may continue to evolve as research advances. Additionally, diagnostic practices can vary by region and may be influenced by cultural factors and available resources.

Symbols

Here are some of the most commonly recognized symbols associated with autism and their origins:

Puzzle Piece:

- The puzzle piece is perhaps the most well-known, and now controversial, symbol for autism awareness. In some representations, it is a multi-colored jigsaw puzzle piece, often with a single missing piece.
- The puzzle piece was first introduced in 1963 by the National Autistic Society (NAS) in the United Kingdom. The design represents the idea that autism is a complex puzzle that society needs to solve to better understand and support individuals with autism.

Autism Awareness Ribbon:

- The Autism Awareness Ribbon consists of a ribbon shape in various colors, with shades of blue being the most common. Blue represents calmness and understanding. In some cases, the puzzle pieces are included with the ribbon.
- The use of ribbons as symbols for various causes has a long history, and the autism awareness ribbon follows this tradition by promoting awareness and support for individuals with autism.
- Infinity Symbol:
- The infinity symbol (∞) has been used to represent autism as well. It signifies the infinite potential and unique abilities of individuals on the autism spectrum.
- The symbol emphasizes the idea that individuals with autism

have diverse talents and abilities that can be nurtured and celebrated.

- Rainbow Color Spectrum and Infinity Symbol:
- Some variations of the infinity symbol incorporate rainbow colors, representing diversity and acceptance within the autism community.
- The rainbow colors symbolize the idea that every person with autism is unique and should be celebrated for their individuality.

Overall, the symbols associated with autism have evolved over time to raise awareness, promote acceptance, and encourage support for individuals on the autism spectrum. It's important to note that different symbols are preferred by different individuals and groups within the autism community.

Terminology

Like the symbols, the terminology used to describe autism and individuals with autism has evolved over time as our understanding of the condition and societal attitudes have changed. Different terms are preferred by different individuals and groups within the autism community, and language choice can be a matter of personal preference. Here are some key terms and their meanings:

- Autism: This is the medical and diagnostic term for the neurodevelopmental condition. It describes a range of conditions characterized by challenges with social skills, repetitive behaviors, and communication differences.
- Person-First Language: (Person with Autism) Person-first language emphasizes the individuality of the person before

their diagnosis. It is intended to put the person before the condition and is often seen as a way to humanize and respect individuals with autism.

- Identity-First Language: (Autistic Person) Identity-first language emphasizes autism as an inherent part of a person's identity. Advocates for identity-first language argue that autism is not something separate from the person but rather an integral aspect of who they are.

- Neurodiversity: This term represents the idea that neurological differences, including autism, should be seen as natural variations in the human population rather than as disorders to be cured. It promotes acceptance and celebrates the diversity of neurotypes.

- High-Functioning Autism (HFA): Older term (prior to DSM-5) used to describe individuals on the autism spectrum who have relatively mild to moderate challenges in communication and daily living skills. However, it is increasingly seen as problematic and oversimplifying, as it does not capture the full range of an individual's abilities and challenges.

- Low-Functioning Autism (LFA): Similar to HFA, this older term (prior to DSM-5) has been used to describe individuals with more significant challenges in communication and daily living skills. It is also seen as overly simplistic and stigmatizing.

- Autistic Traits: This term is used to describe behaviors and characteristics commonly associated with autism. It is often employed when discussing traits or behaviors without labeling individuals as "autistic."

- Spectrum: The term "spectrum" reflects the idea that autism presents in a wide range of ways, with varying degrees of severity and a diverse array of strengths and challenges. It emphasizes the idea that each individual with autism is unique.

- Special Needs: This term has been used to describe individuals with disabilities, including autism. However, some find it overly vague and prefer more specific language to describe the needs of individuals.
- Disability Community: Autism is considered part of the broader disability community, which includes individuals with various disabilities. This term emphasizes solidarity and shared experiences among individuals with different conditions.
- Autistic Self-Advocate: This term describes individuals with autism who actively advocate for themselves and the autism community. These advocates often work to promote understanding, acceptance, and inclusion.
- Stimming (Self-Stimulatory Behavior): This term is used to describe repetitive movements or sounds that some individuals with autism engage in to self-regulate and cope with sensory experiences.

Using Respectful Language

It's important to listen to and respect the language preferences of individuals with autism and the broader autism community. Using respectful language can contribute to greater understanding and acceptance of individuals with autism and promote inclusivity and empathy.

Here are some examples of autism myths and what NOT to do when talking about autism:

- Using Derogatory Language: Using derogatory terms or slurs to describe individuals with autism is highly offensive and perpetuates stigma. Avoid using terms that belittle or demean people with autism.

- Pathologizing Autism: Describing autism solely as a "problem", "disorder", or "disease" without acknowledging the strengths, talents, and unique qualities of autistic individuals. Autism is a neurodivergent identity, and it's important to recognize the positive aspects of neurodiversity.

- Assuming Autism Is a Tragedy: Expressing pity or sorrow upon learning that someone is autistic. Autism is not inherently tragic, and many autistic individuals lead fulfilling and happy lives.

- Using "Normal" as a Benchmark: Implying that autistic individuals are not "normal" or that they should strive to be "normal." Autism is a natural variation of the human experience, and there is no single standard of "normal."

- Underestimating Abilities: Assuming that individuals with autism are incapable or less competent in various areas without giving them a chance to demonstrate their abilities. Autistic individuals have diverse talents and skills.

- Ignoring Accommodations and Support Needs: Neglecting to provide reasonable accommodations or support for autistic individuals in educational, work, or social settings can be discriminatory. It's important to acknowledge and respect their specific needs.

- Labeling Behavior as "Meltdowns" or "Tantrums": Labeling behavior as "meltdowns" or "tantrums" without considering sensory sensitivities, communication challenges, or emotional regulation issues can misrepresent the experiences of autistic individuals. It's crucial to understand the underlying factors contributing to behavior.

- Blaming Autism for All Challenges: Attributing all difficulties or behaviors to autism without considering external factors or individual circumstances can be dismissive and stigmatizing. It's important to recognize that people with autism, like anyone else, can face a wide range of challenges unrelated to their neurodivergent identity.

- Assuming Homogeneity: Treating all autistic individuals as if they are the same or have identical needs and experiences is an oversimplification and can lead to misunderstandings. Autism is a spectrum, and every individual is unique.
- Exclusion or Isolation: Excluding or isolating autistic individuals from social or educational activities based on their neurodivergent status. Inclusion and accessibility should be a priority.

Promoting understanding and respect for autistic individuals involves using inclusive language, recognizing their strengths and contributions, and providing the necessary support and accommodations to ensure their full participation in society. It's essential to listen to and learn from autistic voices and perspectives.

Here are ten examples of respectful language and terminology when talking about autism:

- "Autistic Individual" or "Person with Autism": Use identity-first language, such as "autistic individual" or person-first language, such as "person with autism," as per the individual's preference. This respects their identity while acknowledging their autism.
- "Neurodiverse": Describe individuals with autism as "neurodiverse" to highlight the natural variation in neurological conditions and promote acceptance.
- "Autism Spectrum": Refer to autism as a "spectrum" to emphasize the wide range of abilities, challenges, and characteristics within the autism community.

- "Unique Abilities and Strengths": Highlight the unique abilities and strengths of autistic individuals, such as "exceptional memory," "talented artist," or "passionate advocate."
- "Sensory Sensitivities": Use language that acknowledges sensory sensitivities, such as "sensory-friendly environment" or "accommodations for sensory needs."
- "Autistic Advocates": Recognize and promote the voices of autistic advocates and activists who work to raise awareness and improve the lives of those with autism.
- "Supportive and Inclusive Environment": Emphasize the importance of creating a "supportive and inclusive environment" for autistic individuals in education, work, and community settings.
- "Communication Differences": Respectfully acknowledge "communication differences" rather than labeling difficulties or challenges.
- "Autistic Community": Refer to the community of individuals with autism as the "autistic community" to recognize their shared experiences and connections.
- "Embracing Neurodiversity": Encourage the idea of "embracing neurodiversity" to promote acceptance and inclusion of all neurological variations, including autism.

Respectful language not only demonstrates empathy and understanding but also helps combat stigma and discrimination against individuals with autism. It's important to be attentive to individual preferences regarding language, as some people may have specific preferences for how they wish to be described or identified. Listening to and respecting the choices of autistic individuals regarding their self-identification is a fundamental aspect of respectful communication.

STORY 1:

Rev. Jeannette Paxia
and Jacob Stolle

Rev. Jeannette Paxia
Mom, Advocate, Speaker, Coach, Author, Podcast Host
Favorite Superhero: Wonder Woman

Boom! Boom! Boom!

I could feel my son's pain as he hit his fists on the ground while kicking his feet. A full-blown 2-year-old meltdown, but he was way older and bigger than a 2-year-old. He wanted something in the store, and I had said no. My son, Jacob, doesn't understand social cues, and when he wants something, he wants it now. I honestly didn't care about the stares or what people thought. In fact, I doubt I registered much more than thinking, 'Now what do I do?' Then a lady comes up to me and says, 'Someone needs to beat that child.' It's comments like these that need to change. I am not going to debate whether spanking is okay or not; my point is, keep your opinion to yourself. When you see that there is a parent who is stressed already, he/she doesn't need your opinion to add to the stress. How in the world do you know what he/she has tried or not tried? Why make a situation worse than it is?

At home, everything was a challenge. We had to figure out what worked for Jacob and what didn't. It seemed something would work for a while, and our house would be peaceful, then suddenly it stopped working.

Buying clothes was one of the hardest things. His sensory issues were a major problem. I would buy something; he would say, "Oh yes, this is perfect." and wear it for an hour or a day and then say he couldn't stand the way it felt on his body. Jacob was about 10 when we finally received an autism diagnosis, at that time he was diagnosed with Asperger's. At least with a diagnosis, I could research and learn how to help him. In addition to his autism diagnosis, he was diagnosed with a few other things, including OCDs (Obsessive-compulsive disorders). Every night, I had to read 3 books to him; it couldn't be 1 or 2, it had to be 3. He had to wash his hands for a certain amount of time while tapping his foot. Touching doorknobs was a problem. These are just a small portion of a lens into our world, and I could tell these OCDs were driving him crazy.

For years, school was very stressful; we would get calls about how he was disrupting class again. He was then moved to an alternative school and did well for a bit and then got kicked out of that school. I searched the country for a school that would best suit him, found a highly rated school, and then he was abused there. The challenges were many, and some days, I didn't think we would make it through, but we did.

I would love to share with the world that although Jacob was diagnosed with Autism (and other issues), what I want the world to know is that I am proud to be his mom. A diagnosis is just information that I can use to best support him. It does not make or break him, and it does not define him. We all have things that make us different, and that is okay. He is the most caring person, and every day I find new things about him that amaze me.

My dreams for my child are that after college, he locates work in a field he loves, that he finds happiness with a partner, and that he is able to use his many abilities to serve others. He is finishing his last year at Landmark, a college that supports students with neurodiversity. I found this college by 'accident,' and I could not be happier with how well he is doing there. For a while, I thought he would be working in a field he hated because he didn't do well at a traditional college, but all of that has changed now.

Please do not judge others by what you see; when you see a parent struggling, do not assume they are not a good parent. Do what you can to help them, and that might just be to leave them alone!

> **Find out more about Rev. Jeannette Paxia here:**
>
> www.innersuperhero.org
> www.innersuperhero.me
> Instagram: your_inner_superhero
> TikTok: inner_superhero
> App - Inner Superhero
> Podcast: Ordinary People Extraordinary Lives hosted on Word Of Mom Radio

Jacob Stolle
Autistic Adult, Student, Animal Enthusiast
Favorite Superhero: Spiderman

Why do people look at me and talk to me like I am stupid? Just because I ask questions for clarification does not mean I am ignorant; it's my way of processing. To understand how to react to someone's expression, I must actively think about it. It took a while for me to figure things out, and now that I understand the differences between those with autism and those without, it's easier for me. My view of the world is different than most people's, well, all our views are different no matter who you are, but through my autism, I see things in a way that most neurotypical people don't. I have an innate sense of people and animals, especially animals. Not only do animals calm me down (my emotional support dog, Charlie, has gotten me through a lot), but I can empathize with how they feel. Although socially awkward, I have spent years trying to understand people, figure out how to answer what they are asking, and generally just understanding them. My mom says that my understanding of people far outweighs anyone else she knows.

Finding and starting to attend college was at first nerve-wracking. New things for me initiate anxiety attacks; I like my routine; I like what I know. I had tried a typical college, and it was too difficult with all the students and the expectations. My new college caters to those who have a neurodiverse diagnosis. Once I got used to my new environment, it became and still is an amazing experience. Although I believe that people with a diagnosis of autism need to spend time with neurotypical and neurodiverse people, being around people who understand me is freeing. For the first time, I do not have to try and mask the behaviors that make neurotypical people nervous and uncomfortable. My classmates understand me! My teachers understand me! I can be myself! I have also made a lot of good friends; previously, I had made a couple of friends, but it was harder to do. I now have several close friends. Through the years, I have had some crazy experiences. I am not sure I can identify the hardest of these, but one of the most memorable was living through my OCDs. OCDs, wow, when they are extreme, they can really mess your life up. I remember almost setting the house on fire because I had to have the cereal box a certain distance from the stove. Thankfully, I worked through these, and the worst of them lasted about a year and a half. I would love the world to better understand neurodiverse people. Although we are all different and often one diagnosis usually accompanies others, we shouldn't always be the ones who have to figure everyone else out. You can't always tell if someone is neurodiverse by looking at them, and I understand that can make it more difficult for everyone. If we could all just try and get along with each other and accept people as they are, it would be a lot easier for everyone to get along.

STORY 2:
Dr. Crystal Morrison

Mom, Scientist, Entrepreneur, and Advocate
Favorite Superhero: My children

I went to work every day and held my breath worrying that daycare would call. Did he bite another child? Did he throw a chair in class? Would I have to clear my schedule again? What am I doing wrong? These questions were always punching me in the gut. My child was an inquisitive, imaginative sweetheart 95% of the time. He was an absolute joy. The other 5% of the time, he was untethered. The triggers were various. Another child venturing into his sacred sphere. A crack in his cereal bar. Another child playing loudly with a toy. Any change in schedule, especially mealtime and nap time. Being told to sit quietly and color - that was a recipe for disaster (as was the entire year he had the teacher that preferred students to sit quietly and color).

Many people know the exact date and time they received their child's autism diagnosis. I do not.

Something seemed different when he arrived in the world. As a new mom, my concerns were cast off as overreacting. He was a very colicky baby and screamed from 6 p.m. until midnight for the first 12 weeks. My sleep-deprived body barely functioned but my carpet was clean because the sound of a vacuum cleaner was the only thing that calmed him. His schedule was sacred. If we deviated from nap or food by more than 5-10 minutes, hell would break loose. Once he got teeth, he enforced his boundaries by biting anyone in his vicinity and one child became his "chomp of choice." As he grew into toddlerhood, the aggression increased, and preschool chairs were frequently airborne. Changes in schedule or unexpected deviations from what had been forewarned were met by an inquisition and often an unraveling. His favorite teacher left the preschool program and he immediately regressed on potty training for a whole year.

The toddler and preschool years also revealed his gifts. My son could talk in complete sentences and carry on an intelligent conversation with adults. As a toddler, he knew every engine character by name in the Thomas the Tank Engine series and could share details about the engine design. The preschool years brought an intense interest in the space shuttle, and everything related to solid rocket boosters and external fuel tanks. Other children really didn't interest him, and even adult conversations might bring disappointment. Once an adult told him that the "moon was made of cheese." He was immediately mortified and informed the man that it was "impossible for the moon to be made of cheese" and that the moon is "actually made of rock and orbits the earth." He also told the man that his mommy (me) taught him about the moon. He was 4. He was also gifted two large containers of Legos with no instructions, and they became the gift that kept giving for no less than 10 more years. His mind saw images and structures and his hands created them, being disrupted only by forced bathroom and food breaks. His focus was unrivaled if something interested him.

Starting school brought new challenges and expectations of conformity. Sitting at a desk, following specific directions, and staying in the lines were just not conceivable to my child. Moving around the floor, having detailed conversations, making rocket noises, and playing alone were all more his speed. He was often excluded from birthday parties and kicked out of gymnastics class because he was too 'rowdy.' Other kids avoided him because they didn't understand what he was talking about. Holding a pencil and writing became a significant challenge. His brain was moving so fast and channeling those thoughts into words on paper seemed impossible and massively frustrating.

Even though the classroom felt restrictive, he quickly inhaled the knowledge around him. As he started picking up on letters, words, and sentences, there was no stopping him. He read the entire Harry Potter series by the time he was eight years old and hasn't stopped reading voraciously since. I never limited his interests, maybe because many were like mine. The airplane and space phase was one of my favorites as I had always dreamed of being an astronaut or fighter pilot as a child. He took the interest a step further and could identify all US military aircraft and their associated manufacturers. I adored those long airplane discussions.

While I adored those conversations, I knew the rest of the world didn't see my son's gifts. The rest of the world saw a socially awkward little boy with an adult vocabulary and violent meltdowns. Observers commented on my lack of "good parenting skills" and often suggested that "a good spanking" would "line him out." Observers judged me. They judged him. They decided he and I didn't fit in the "OK" box and that we were the problem.

In 2012, we moved across the United States to Pennsylvania. There were many reasons for the move and a significant benefit was more resources and opportunities for my children. The public school system was instrumental in connecting me with the right people for evaluations. Amid the piles of paper was the word "autism" along with multiple other diagnoses. There was nothing earth-shattering about the words because I already knew, and the words had been mentioned for years. The only difference was that the words were on the right forms at the right time in the right place to open the right doors. The "autism" word was a key. I would love to say that having the key and opening up more resources solved everything, but you and I know that's not true. We had an array of therapists of every variety, teachers, classroom support services, and IEPs (Individualized Education Plans). Our "village" was significant. All these resources were critical and helpful, but we couldn't hold off the tide of my son's growth, hormones, and increasing volatility. His teenage years also brought more trauma on top of an already complex situation. There were times I feared him and believed jail time might be part of his future.

We all worked so hard together as a family and my son worked especially hard. While in high school, he surprised me and expressed interest in getting a part-time job. Along with therapy, his work experience was significant in building confidence, personal responsibility and reinforcing important skills. His employer frequently hires individuals with various disabilities, and it was (and still is) an incredibly supportive and inclusive atmosphere with excellent management and staff. I admit that I was very doubtful about him working. I was terrified he would be triggered by a customer or employee interaction. I was worried he would get lost in thought and cause an accident. I was concerned he would not be able to follow directions. I'm delighted that he proved me wrong and blossomed into a valued employee. As of this writing, my son is trying out college and independent living with his adored fat cat Sylvester. I don't know what his future holds, but I can assure you, we will continue to celebrate all the wins along the way.

Recently, I asked my son what he would like the world to know about autism and he said, "It's not what you think. Most people have a perception of autism from TV and media, like Sheldon from Big Bang Theory. Yes, Sheldon's character is likely autistic but he's only one limited example of autism. I told someone once that I'm autistic and their response was 'You don't look autistic.' What's that supposed to mean? I guess I didn't wear my autism costume that day." As a parent, I also want people to give each other grace and support. When that parent and child are struggling, refrain from judgment. If you feel compelled, you can simply ask, "Is there anything I can do the help you right now?" There may be nothing you can do but the offer will at least make that parent and child feel seen and supported.

My journey alongside my autistic son has been filled with challenges that have tested my strength and patience but also allowed growth and new perspectives. Through his struggles and triumphs, my son has given me the invaluable gift of seeing the world through a different lens. As I look back on our journey, I am filled with gratitude for the remarkable person my son has become and the village of support we've had to get to where we are now. Our story is one of challenges, yes, but it is also a story of acceptance, resilience, grace, and the enduring power of unconditional love.

And we still love to talk about airplanes.

Find out more about Dr. Crystal Morrison here:

www.meerkatvillage.com
www.thevillagevision.com
LinkedIn: https://www.linkedin.com/in/drcrystalmorrison/

STORY 3:
Lynn Arthur

Mom, Advocate
Favorite Superhero: Elastigirl and Dash from the Incredibles

Opening the screen door of the kitchen, he flung his backpack onto the table. The first middle school year was coming to an end. Since survival mode was the norm for the last 6 years, drama and intensity were comforting. We operated at one speed. GO GO GO.... crash! GO GO GO. There was no warning for the 'meltdown.' It was likely predictable, but since I was also living in survival mode, I had no bandwidth to recognize when things were too much. They always seemed too much.

Both boys had made it home after school. Usually, we had a little window of downtime after school. The kitchen door swung open and as fast as lightning he ran down the street toward the woods. With a 9-year-old sitting in the kitchen and an 11-year-old bolting down the street on a tear, I had to make a calculated choice. Looking back, I should have 'let him run.' He had wandered off before just to get out and get into nature and he made his way back. This time there was rage and fear present.

Full sprint down the street into the woods, dodging branches, hurdling rocks. It felt like a scene from 'The Hunger Games' or almost cartoon-like. At some point, he tripped over a broken wire fence. I was able to catch up and found myself preventing him from repeatedly hitting his head against a big rock. I scooped him up and carried him home while restraining him with my arms wrapped around him. I honestly don't know if I made it worse by chasing him, but his logical thinking was impaired by his adrenalized response to whatever he was running from in his head.

A story unfolded about being stuck in a school locker. It was a detailed, elaborate story. I bought it 'hook, line, and sinker'. You can imagine the anger of a mother whose son struggles with friendships and social interactions and was shut in his locker for 3 periods by his friends.

No action from the school. WHAT?? GRRRR. Mama Bear was in full effect. When you are clouded by anxiety and fear and survival, you lock onto the story and you fight for your child.

He was calling for help, not because his friends had locked him in a locker, but because he had locked himself in a locker.

It took a few years before I learned that truth. In the meantime, I took up the same strategy that he had, I ran. I quit my job so that he could finish the school year at home with tutoring, gave notice to my landlord of our 3-bedroom apartment, and we moved into a 300-square-foot studio apartment over a friend's garage. The boys started new schools. I wish I could say that things swung in a good direction, but it was a roller coaster, a lonely, shameful, destructive roller coaster of survival. It perpetually felt like we were in survival mode. And indeed, we were.

For him, school was intolerable. He just shut down, hid behind his hair, and withdrew. He appeared as though he didn't care and wasn't listening. All along, he was listening. He knew that if he shut down, he would be able to focus on the teacher's voice and words. He retained all the information he heard. He never had to study and tested well. The problem was that he didn't see the purpose of homework, was pretty spent from keeping it together at school, and didn't tolerate being in the classrooms. So much noise!

Over the years, he had innately developed strategies to self-regulate. Those first few years were rough and honestly full of shame and guilt. I was just trying to help him survive. We began to learn what caused stress and triggered him. It was never just one thing. It was a build-up. We started making decisions about activities that were more agreeable to his nervous system. We started to understand and influence what routines and strategies to implement when it seemed his cup was overflowing. So, we took cues from the strategies he was developing and found ways to support those self-regulation techniques.

From a very early age, he took an obsessive liking to Legos. He would spend hours focused and creating. He called himself a Lego engineer. He would set a timer and beat the suggested time for building. He would create new ships and structures without instructions. The thousands of dollars invested and occasionally stepping on a misplaced Lego piece seemed worth the therapeutic benefits.

He also found great freedom and ease when in nature. He was my hiker. At 10 years old, he could hike 4,000 footers in New Hampshire. He liked the physicality and got lost in all of the sensory stimulation found in nature. He loved swimming in rivers and the ocean. He would fully submerge himself and get instant ease from the cold and pressure of the water. When he didn't have access to bodies of water, he would take showers with his clothes on and cover himself in towels. He loved the pressure of the wet heavy cold towels. It was a mess, but it calmed him instantly.

What I didn't know in the first few years was why the strategies he chose were so effective. Being the nerd I am, I did a deep dive into neuroscience. This is where I found that nature and cold water, running to exhaustion, the pressure of weighted wet towels, and obsessive control over creating Lego forms were all effective strategies to self-regulate.

He knew what his body needed.

The choice of high school was based on the environment and schedule demand. Finding a school that prioritized less rigid seating arrangements, encouraged on-the-fly problem-solving, and fostered the freedom to move and interact appeared to be crucial. He applied to a tech high school where he chose to turn his strengths in spatial and structural awareness with Legos into a career in plumbing.

Even as an adult, he continues to face the same triggers, the social demands, the schedule demands, and the physical demands. These challenges require him to use the three strategies he discovered 14 years ago to navigate the world, make meaningful contributions, and find a sense of purpose. When he needs to recharge, he ventures into nature and enjoys fishing, hiking, and golf. In the summer, he spends a lot of time submerged in the ocean. He still uses cold showers to get going and recalibrate after work. He is still a Lego aficionado and still 'checks out' and builds for hours…or weekends. He also takes great pride in being able to come up with creative and effective plumbing solutions in these old New England homes. Throughout his life, he has willingly taken on numerous self-imposed challenges as a way to escape some of the chaos and noise that this world can bring. Through these trials and tribulations, he has discovered who he is, what his body needs, and how to thrive in this world.

STORY 4:
Karye Brockert

Mom, Advocate, Educator
Favorite Superhero: My mom

Our autism journey began when my husband and I received the official autism diagnosis for our daughter, Maddie, at the age of 3. This diagnosis was a significant turning point in our lives, both personally and professionally, with the uncertainty looming over us.

At that time, both my husband and I were educators. I was a kindergarten teacher, and he was a football coach. The diagnosis spurred us to make life-changing decisions. We were determined to help other families facing similar challenges, educators like us, and parents who, like ourselves, were navigating the world of autism.

Our journey has been marked by various challenges, but the first, and perhaps most significant, was accepting and embracing the autism diagnosis. Although we suspected autism, labeling our child with ASD, OCD, and severe anxiety was a profound moment.

Maddie's struggles extended beyond her diagnosis. From the time she was born, she had difficulty with sleep, and it was extremely hard to console her as a baby. She experienced colic, acid reflux, and rotavirus, leaving my husband and I wearing bags under our eyes and running on fumes just to navigate daily life. As Maddie was our only child, we lacked a frame of reference to compare her development. I had diligently read all the books on what to expect, but reality proved to be quite different. In many ways, our experiences could have contributed to a new book titled "What Not to Expect!"

One of the most distressing memories is from when Maddie was just a toddler. She had a high fever and was utterly lethargic. Taking her to the pediatrician turned into a nightmare. The nurses were puzzled because Maddie, despite feeling unwell, was remarkably active in resisting their efforts. They began by checking her ears, but it was a difficult task due to the wax build-up, which needed to be removed. For a child with sensory issues, you can imagine how uncomfortable and overwhelming that must have been. Once her ears were clear, the medical team suspected strep throat and subjected her to a throat swab, another invasive and uncomfortable procedure. When the strep test was returned as negative, they finally decided to test for the flu. By then, the cries of distress could likely be heard in the next town! When they inserted that long swab up her tiny nose for the flu test, Maddie screamed in a way I had never heard before. The test confirmed she had swine flu.

Following that traumatic experience, Maddie's trust in us was shattered. She became so distrustful that we couldn't even ride in the same car, as she would attempt to escape in fear. Driving past the doctor's office or uttering any medical terms would send her into a state of extreme anxiety. Maddie was diagnosed with post-traumatic stress disorder (PTSD) and was prescribed various medications.

With time, her anxiety became somewhat more manageable as she regained some of her trust. Yet, she remains extremely fearful of any medical appointment or procedure.

We enrolled Maddie in a developmental preschool. Her preschool years were marked by her ability to exhibit splinter skills that amazed us. She could read, identify composers of instrumental pieces, count by twos, and even recite the alphabet backward. However, she had a difficult time regulating her emotions, exhibited challenging behaviors, and struggled with communication. The stress and exhaustion took a toll on our ability to work.

During these trying times, my mother, Maddie's grandmother, emerged as my superhero. She was the only one I could trust completely and confide in, and she sacrificed more than words can express to provide us with the invaluable help and unwavering support that we needed. She became our anchor in the storm, the constant source of strength that guided us through the challenges of Maddie's journey.

As Maddie reached middle school and all the fun that puberty brings, we decided to homeschool her, where her anxiety could be better managed. This shift was remarkably successful, as we could achieve in 30 minutes what previously took an entire school day.

As we navigated life, my husband and I discovered our passion. I pursued a second master's degree in special education, eventually leading me to my current role as the director at Easterseals Academy. Meanwhile, my husband embarked on a journey to law school, becoming an attorney who represents parents of special needs children.

During this time, I assumed the position as the director of Easterseals Academy, a private K-12 school for students with special needs. My personal passion fueled the desire to create a school environment tailored to students like Maddie. I wanted parents like us to feel confident when dropping their children off at school, knowing they are safe and loved, and all their needs are met. I also strived to provide direct support to educators on best practices in special education.

As Maddie grew into her high school years, her fears took on a new dimension. She became terrified of the concept of aging and death, which is profoundly challenging to understand and explain. Now, she doesn't want anyone to discuss dates on a calendar or anything related to the passage of time, as it signifies moving closer to the unknown of death.

Maddie is now 17 and still struggles with intense anxiety but we have found our way in this journey with her as our tour guide. Maddie has such inspirational qualities. She possesses the purest of souls, and her nature is genuinely kind. She has a unique and delightful sense of humor that never fails to brighten our days. In a world that often needs more individuals like Maddie, she stands as a shining example.

What I hope the world understands about people living with autism is the importance of awareness and inclusion. Autism is not something to fear or view negatively. It's about accepting differences and fostering an environment where autism is understood without needing explanations. The behaviors observed are simply a form of communication.

One of my greatest sources of pride is the courage and resilience my daughter exhibits daily. She works hard to achieve what comes naturally to most, facing challenges that are often taken for granted. Like any parent, our dreams for the future revolve around Maddie living as independently as possible, knowing that she will thrive, and the world will embrace her for the remarkable individual she is, celebrating her differences.

Find out more about Karye Brockert here:

LinkedIn: https://www.linkedin.com/in/karye-brockert/

STORY 5:
Kelly Cain

Mom, Advocate

Favorite Superhero: My Children

Back in 2006, when my son received his autism diagnosis, I could never have imagined the remarkable journey it would lead us on. The day he was diagnosed was a significant one in our home.

Initially, we were informed that he might never develop verbal speech. As he entered first grade, he still had not made progress in this area. For many parents, sending their children to school can feel like a lifeline, a hope that somehow school will "fix it." However, our experience quickly showed us that the reality was quite different. School was navigating uncharted waters, just as we were. This was an incredibly challenging time for our family, especially for him.

In school, the behaviors from frustration in communication crept in (hiding under a desk). Once he did start to talk, the social challenges, including misreading of social cues by him and the uneducated around him lead to behaviors that were not appropriate. When the behaviors became overwhelming, we were told he needed a specialized school.

It was heartbreaking and, in my mind, unacceptable.

We took him for another evaluation.

With this diagnosis, unlike others, we were constantly getting different opinions on therapy and adjustments. In addition, his performance in different classes was very different, but it also helped us better understand him. He would be an angel in social studies and have a "meltdown in math." It was hard for us to send him to school and miserable for him. I am sure he wore a mask and smiled for most. Staff would always reassure me how "nice" everyone was to him. One counselor said at every meeting that "the kids are so nice to him." I always thought, "shouldn't they always be nice to him?" I think 1st grade was a great year for him. Looking back, the teacher "got it." The aide "got it." There was one girl in his class who insisted on helping him, and maybe even at that young age she "got it."

During an evaluation, my husband came in a little late after working on a roof. He was a little frantic thinking he may have missed the "update." The psychiatrist looked at both of us and said your son needs a private education that can cost more than a year at college. My husband and I both knew that scenario was impossible. The silence was deafening. Financially, we had initially planned our future with both incomes. However, this plan came to a halt five years prior due to the diagnosis. I can tell you that the financial strain may have caused even more worry than the diagnosis itself. One of us had to be there. We didn't go without, but it wasn't as comfortable for us.

We were informed his local school would be financially responsible for the specialized school, but after touring, we decided the commute would be difficult and adjustments could be made at his school. The local school adjusted. We adjusted. Team meetings, communication logs, training, phone calls, and adjusted schedules all became part of my day, every day. I learned the acronym IEP and all its power. He graduated with his neurotypical peers. I was so happy when he graduated because I knew the anxiety he felt.

By the way, all those "nice kids" never invited him to a birthday party or graduation party. One "nice kid" did come to his graduation party.

Now, after 2 1/2 years of trying different jobs and social opportunities, college will be part of his story. At his suggestion, he has decided to go to college. I went with him to tour the school and applied for the parent plus loan. I went with him to meet his counselors. I was listening to them as they questioned him about his likes and dislikes. I wondered if they "get it." Are they trained? Do they understand what it took to get here?   I sat there trying not to answer for him. Occasionally, he would glance at me with his eyebrows raised, twirling something in his hand and wondering. He gives me this look when he is unsure of the question and is looking at me to rephrase the question for him. I sat there silently. In this part of his story, there will be no communication logs, no team meetings to adjust work or schedules. There will be no "touring for outside placements" if he doesn't fit.

I will not know if the kids are "nice to him."

My wish is that he is invited to parties and that he advocates for himself to staff. My wish is that at least one person becomes a friend.

My wish is that this chapter of his story lights him up inside and that he finds joy.

My wish is That he finds acceptance amongst his peers and the world he enters "gets him."

Find out more about Kelly Cain here:

www.autismcaringcenter.com
https://www.linkedin.com/in/kelly-cain-73b43a14b/

STORY 6:
Carrie Cariello

Mom, Author, and Advocate
Favorite Superhero: My children

I wanted to hug you tonight.

I saw you walk in the door, and I tried my best to smile. But I just couldn't bring myself to reach for you. I can't explain why.

After all, we embraced this morning. It was light, and easy. It suggested a good day ahead.

The problem is a lot has happened since 7:00 am.

Adolescent arguments, remote learning at the kitchen table, long phone calls about an overdue prescription.

Then there were the snacks.

Crumbs on the counter, cups in the sink.

I wanted to hug you.

I wanted to feel your arms around me and nestle my head into the space I have nestled for nearly twenty-five years.

But I didn't.

I guess you could say life interfered, and the tedium chipped away at any goodwill I might have held close.

It's not your fault.

It just is.

I thought about you at work, laughing with patients and solving problems and doing important things.

I know it's not that simple.

It's hard to feel as though my work is important.

It is the work of details, and sameness.

Laundry, grocery shopping, cooking, folder-sorting, space-making.

I know. It's not that simple.

Every now and again, when I'm folding hooded sweatshirts and extra-long pants, I remember their sweet toddler faces. I think of their chubby cheeks, and wide smiles, and I am overcome with sadness.

I wanted to hug you when you walked in the door.

But autism got in the way.

Jack had a half day at school. He wanted to go out for lunch. He chose a small restaurant in town, the one that serves his favorite chicken tenders.

On the way there he fiddled with the radio, and I snapped at him.

Jack! Please, just find a song.

As soon as we got out of the car, I reminded him to stay with me in the parking lot.

We walked inside and I held his elbow so he wouldn't move past the hostess stand to sit at the counter.

We always sit at the counter.

The server came to take our drink order, and I tried to catch her eye. I wanted to send an invisible signal to let her know why he was looking down, and hesitating before he spoke.

I've been doing these things for so long; I don't even notice anymore.

Wait. Yes, I do.

Yes, I do.

I notice.

I notice all the time.

And I hate it.

I hate that he checks with me before he orders another soda with his lunch.

But he would easily drink four at a time and I'm pretty sure all the sugar and caffeine interacts somehow with his medication because he doesn't seem to sleep as well.

Our son takes medication.

I can hardly believe it myself.

I hate the look of recognition people get in their eyes when they realize—a-ha!—he has special needs.

They usually can't quite place it at first.

Why does he fidget like that?

Why does he take so long to order?

Why does he pause, and look down, and twitch his fingers?

Our son has special needs.

I can hardly believe it myself.

Our grief is separate, like bright buckets of paint we carry.

Mine overflows with scarlet red and searing yellow. It is messy, and loud. It fills the room.

Your grief, well, it's contained. You hold it close. It is dark, and cloudy, like so many shades of grey and black.

We both hope for him, it's true.

My hope feels like a bag of rocks strapped to my back. I shift it from my hip to my shoulders, always uncomfortable beneath the weight.

Your hope is more like a bolt of lightning. It keeps you moving. It propels you forward.

When it misses the mark, the burn is bright, and hot.

Desperately, we are trying to piece together what it takes to raise this boy into a man.

My work is day-to-day. I remind him to say please in the restaurant and to use his napkin. I make sure his medicine is refilled and watch carefully for any interactions. I make sure he has the right wipes to keep his glasses clean.

You tackle the bigger things—religion, budgeting money, how to hang lights on the Christmas tree.

I wanted to hug you tonight.

But so much happened since this morning.

I made a three-pound meatloaf for dinner. I don't even like meatloaf.

I noticed a long scratch on my desk that wasn't from me.

I drove to the pharmacy and showed my license so I could pick up his vial of small, white pills.

These tiny slights build up and they start to ring inside my mind, like loose change inside a ceramic bowl.

I am never alone.

And yet, I am lonely.

Now, more than ever, I need you to be my witness.

Yes, I yelled about the crumbs on the counter. But I also held them tight when they had nightmares. I bought the apples they liked.

I tried. Please, tell them how much I tried.

Remind me of the days when I thought I had nothing more to give— when I was completely tapped out and I had no energy and could not soothe another angry teenager or sign another form—remind me that I dug as deep as I could for them.

I am digging as deep as I can.

I take nothing for granted.

Building a family is important work.

It is fast, and fiery, and special, and ordinary.

I ache for what was.

I'm often dissatisfied with what is.

And I fear what may become.

I wanted to hug you tonight.

Together, we root for him.

We stand side-by-side and with all our might, we root for this boy.

Maybe that's enough.

It has to be enough.

You taught him how to pray.

I love you, fiercely and forever.

Find out more about Carrie Cariello here:

www.carriecariello.com
Facebook: Carrie Cariello

Carrie is the Amazon Best Selling author of "What Color Is Monday, How Autism Changed One Family for the Better," "Someone I'm With Has Autism," and her latest book, "Half My Sky, Autism, Marriage, and the Messiness that is Building a Family"

STORY 7:

Angela Chapes

Autism and Mental Health Advocate
Favorite Superhero: My Mom

I am an individual with autism along with co-occurring mental illnesses including obsessive-compulsive disorder, depression, and anxiety. I am a client support provider which is a Case Manager and Peer Support combined where I work at a community mental health center. I have developed a strong sense of self and thick emotional skin through this organization. Some days are challenging but my job is still rewarding.

My journey on the autism spectrum began in my twenties. Unlike some, I was not diagnosed as a child. Instead, I had various diagnoses that didn't quite capture my unique struggles and qualities. My early years were marked by being labeled with defiant disorder, learning disabilities, and math difficulties. Speech therapy and counseling were integral to my development as I grappled with behavioral issues. However, I must emphasize the pivotal role my mother played during this tumultuous period.

My mom, my biggest supporter and superhero, never gave up on me, even when my behavior was at its most challenging. I expressed my frustration and anger through destructive actions, such as throwing and breaking toys or screaming at my family members. I had moments of recklessness, even endangering my brother. My mom's unwavering belief in me and her relentless support kept me from taking a darker path. Her love and determination were the guiding lights that prevented me from ending up in juvenile detention or worse.

My path to self-understanding was not straightforward. It was filled with hurdles, misdiagnoses, and struggles with behavior. My father, though well-intentioned, had a strict parenting style that, at times, made me feel like a bad person. My mother's presence helped temper my behavior, preventing it from escalating further. While my father and I had our challenges, he tried his best, given his own difficult childhood.

One of my significant milestones was entering college, a feat I achieved despite not doing well on the ACT. My mother's determination came to the fore as she fought for my inclusion in a pilot program at a university. This program allowed me to attend classes with my own accommodations in the university's resource room. I adapted by converting my notes into test questions and studying ahead of time. I also became proactive, consistently asking instructors questions, regardless of how trivial they seemed. My message to others is simple, 'Never hesitate to ask questions.' Your voice deserves to be heard.

Life post-college posed its own set of challenges. I lost my mother to dementia, a devastating blow that left me feeling lost and vulnerable. Simultaneously, I was facing bullying and self-doubt. These combined factors led to a period of deep introspection and struggle. However, my story took a turn for the better, thanks to the superheroes I discovered in my life.

I found my first superheroes in a consumer-run organization, which provided me with a job I excelled at – peer support. Peer support entails individuals with lived experiences sharing their stories to help others facing similar challenges. In this role, I found purpose and a profound sense of fulfillment.

My mentors within the consumer-run organization transformed from friends to invaluable guides in my life. One became a father figure, and the other, a grandmother figure. Their unwavering belief in me, their mentorship, and their continued presence in my life have been instrumental in my growth.

Through my work with mental health, I found a job at a community mental health center that became a haven to me where my superhero traits emerged. I helped individuals navigate crises, find housing, offer support during their most trying moments, and develop bonds along the way as a client support provider. Case Management is where I delve deeper into helping individuals.

Throughout my journey, I've encountered numerous hurdles, but one of my most significant successes has been overcoming the odds and creating a life that I cherish. My involvement in these organizations has revealed hidden talents, such as bookkeeping, that I never thought I possessed. I even rose to the position of assistant director, where I made important decisions and contributed positively to the organization. I found I can handle a lot of stress and be calm in stressful situations such as someone having a seizure.

I eventually decided to explore new horizons and advocate for others. I joined organizations like "Toastmasters International" (www.toastmasters.org), "NAMI (National Alliance on Mental Illness) Kansas" (https://namikansas.org/), and "Autism Society - The Heartland" (https://www.asaheartland.org/). These organizations have been instrumental in my growth as an advocate. Toastmasters International, in particular, I feel, helped me overcome my fear of public speaking. I went from being terrified to giving speeches in front of large audiences, to learning how to speak in front of audiences even when scared. I even delivered a speech via Zoom to parents in Malaysia, a significant milestone in my advocacy journey.

My overarching message to parents and caregivers is never to give up on their children. Every family is unique, and every individual has their own distinctive characteristics. The journey may be challenging, but with the right support and resources, children and adults on the autism spectrum can achieve remarkable things.

The importance of support cannot be overstated. Parents, mentors, and organizations played pivotal roles in my life, transforming me from a loner to someone who values and cherishes lasting friendships. It took time and persistence, but I learned that I am deserving of love and friendship.

Throughout my journey, I've discovered the incredible power of words. Words can hurt deeply, but they can also inspire and heal. It's crucial to be mindful of the words we use, as they can leave a lasting impact. I've also learned not to let others define who I am or what I can achieve. Self-belief is a potent force in shaping our destinies.

My journey on the autism spectrum has been a rollercoaster ride filled with challenges, growth, and moments of profound self-discovery. Through the unwavering support of my family, mentors, and various organizations, I've transformed from a child with behavioral issues into an autism and mental health advocate.

I want my story to serve as a beacon of hope for parents and individuals facing similar challenges. No matter the obstacles, there is always a way forward. Seek help, ask questions, and never give up. Embrace the uniqueness of each individual, for it is our differences that make the world a richer and more beautiful place.

In closing, my journey has taught me the importance of love, support, and believing in oneself. I hope my story inspires others to embark on their own paths of self-discovery and advocacy, knowing that they too have the power to overcome adversity and create a life filled with purpose and fulfillment.

Find out more about Angela Chapes here:

LinkedIn: https://www.linkedin.com/in/
angela-chapes-ba062564/

STORY 8:
Nicky Cuesta

Mom, Advocate

Favorite Superhero: My son

I successfully carried my pregnancy to full term, and on July 15, 2005, my one and only son, Vicente Nicholas Cuesta, came into the world. He was a handsome little boy who brought immense joy to my life. At that moment, my sole mission was clear, to raise him into a respectable individual with good manners and a sense of purpose.

As Vicente grew and began to come into his own, signs of something unusual emerged during his time in Pre-K. His teachers noticed issues with his speech and expressed their concerns. This marked the beginning of our journey to find answers.

After several months of evaluations, it became apparent that Vicente needed ear tubes to address his hearing problems. Once the procedure was completed, we believed that everything would be fine. Gradually, Vicente started showing signs of improvement. His hearing improved, which in turn enhanced his speech, allowing him to communicate more effectively with others. As time went by, Vicente entered the third grade and encountered difficulties with bullies at school. Despite his soft-spoken nature and cheerful demeanor, he began feeling out of place among his classmates. Social cues were a mystery to him, making it challenging to navigate friendships and relationships.

Witnessing my son experience such negativity at a young age was heart-wrenching. I hadn't anticipated that the same issues I witnessed during my school days would still exist. I had hoped that parents and society would be more vigilant in addressing these issues and ensuring a better future for our children.

Once again, teachers expressed concerns about Vicente's ability to focus on his schoolwork. He often appeared distant, lost in his thoughts. Vicente's refuge from the world was his passion for drawing, a way for him to brighten others' days. However, his struggles with social awareness persisted, and it was clear that we needed external help to understand and address these challenges.

Vicente underwent another round of evaluations, this time more intensive. We consulted with specialists, counselors, psychologists, and others. Eventually, Vicente was finally diagnosed with what was called at the time Asperger's syndrome or high functioning autism. Asperger's syndrome is characterized by specific social and behavioral traits, including difficulties in social interactions, repetitive behaviors, limited interests, challenges in understanding emotions, a strong preference for rules and routines, and language and communication difficulties.

The diagnosis was a lot to process, but it helped make sense of Vicente's experiences. Regardless of the label, Vicente remained the same incredible individual with a boundless heart and a deep passion for creativity, games, and curiosity. It was all starting to make sense and fall into place.

A difficult decision loomed ahead, whether to disclose his diagnosis to him. It was a choice I grappled with for months. I took steps to ensure Vicente received the necessary support at school through an Individualized Education Program (IEP), a collaborative effort involving professionals, educators, parents, and sometimes the student to tailor education to the individual's needs. Ultimately, I chose not to define my son by a label or diagnosis. I didn't want him to view it as a barrier to achieving his dreams. It was crucial to me that he knew he was amazing, capable of success, and defined by his efforts to conquer life's challenges and blessings.

Over the years, Vicente continued to face social challenges with his peers. However, with the growth of support services and the strong foundation of support at home, these difficulties gradually diminished. He poured his focus into his work and his passion for the arts, eventually becoming an early coder with a keen interest in game creation.

Fast-forward to high school and Vicente thrived after gaining admission to a local charter school. It felt like a blessing sent directly from above, as many families had tried unsuccessfully to secure a spot there. My faith had led me to this opportunity, and my prayers had been answered.

Throughout his school years, Vicente never questioned why he was taken out of classes or why evaluations were a regular part of his school life. Until one day after an IEP meeting in his junior year, at the age of 16, Vicente finally asked if he was autistic. I had prepared myself for this moment. I explained to him that he had been diagnosed with Asperger's and what it entailed. His immediate response was, "Why didn't you tell me?" I told him that I never wanted him to define himself by a label or diagnosis. Despite feeling different from his friends and family, Vicente had always received the love and support he needed. While he may still have questions as he continues to discover himself, I am confident that he will continue to thrive and be ready for whatever answers come his way. After a few hours of reflecting on the last 16 years of his life, his final thought was that he was thankful that he was never treated differently by those closest to him because of his diagnosis. As parents, we don't know if the decisions we make are the best ones. I just went with my gut on this decision, and I am glad that I did. If you are a parent facing this type of decision, it is up to you.

Parenting a child with autism spectrum disorder (ASD) can be both rewarding and challenging. Here are five suggested ways to support your child's growth and development:

- Early Intervention and Professional Support: Seek early intervention services and work with a team of professionals, including speech therapists, occupational therapists, and behavioral therapists, who specialize in autism spectrum disorders.

- Structured and Predictable Environment: Create a structured daily routine and use visual aids to help your child understand expectations and reduce anxiety.

- Social Skills Training: Enroll your child in social skills training programs and encourage socialization in controlled settings to improve their interaction with peers.

- Effective Communication: Develop communication strategies tailored to your child's needs, including visual support and clear, concise instructions.

- Embrace Their Interests: Support and encourage your child's intense interests, as they can be a source of motivation, engagement, and as a bridge for learning and connection.

With these strategies and unwavering love and support, your child can continue to thrive and overcome the challenges they may encounter on their journey.

Find out more about Nicky Cuesta here:

www.buildingleadershipmindset.com
https://link.creedpro.co/widget/bookings/virtualcoffee30

STORY 9:
Nicole DeWard

Mom, Advocate

Favorite Superhero: My children

As a young mom of four kids, I never imagined having two children with special needs, my firstborn, Bekah, having Down Syndrome, and my second, Jacob, on the autism spectrum. I remember feeling concerned about Jacob's development but had convinced myself he was imitating his sister. Hearing the word "autism" scared me because the "spectrum" was so vast. What would this mean for Jacob's future? I was already grieving Bekah's uncertain future, and then, at the age of 18 months, I found myself pondering Jacob's future as well. All of this was happening while taking care of a newborn baby boy and adopting a five-year-old girl into our family. It was overwhelming, yet my husband and I felt like we were called 'for such a time as this'. Our lives had been surrendered to God at a young age and only grew stronger each day, both personally and together, as a united married couple and parents.

I believe every mom who has a child with special needs has a 'moment' when we feel so ill-equipped for the journey ahead. I had one on a family vacation in 2006 when Jacob was three. As I was putting him to bed one night, he was off in his own world as was his usual tendency. I was encouraging him to interact with me and look me in the eyes to say goodnight. He felt so far away yet he was right in my arms. I snuggled him and cried as he continued to babble to himself and look off into the distance. "Jacob," I asked tearfully, "can you see I'm crying? These tears are because I want you to be with me." He finally made eye contact with me and started laughing at my tears. My heart was so broken. I knew that he didn't understand what he was doing or how it was hurting me. This was autism. The disorder takes my son's attention and captures his brain in a way that causes him to isolate himself and not be socially appropriate because he's not able to observe his surroundings. I continued to observe this through elementary, middle, high school, and now college.

Upon the encouragement of a fellow mom who had two sons on the spectrum, we decided to try the gluten and dairy-free diet. I truly didn't think we could ever do it because bread and cheese were Jacob's main foods. We knew that for it to work, we all had to be on the same page. So, as a family of six, we all jumped in and went gluten and dairy-free for a full year. It was tough but so worth it. Focusing on healthy habits of diet, hydration, exercise, and sleep all play a huge part in regulating the energy in the brain. Not only did we see huge improvements for Jacob, but we saw them for Bekah as well. Honestly, our whole family benefited because so many things were removed from our house.

At the end of elementary and into middle school, we tried medications to help the dysregulation in Jacob's brain, yet it took so much of his bubbly personality. The side effects did not outweigh the benefits. In middle school, we were introduced to Nutrition Response Testing (NRT), which uncovered the dysfunction in his organ systems that was contributing to Jacob's symptoms and burdens on his body. While we may not ever be able to 'cure' autism, I do believe we can support the body in a way that helps to live an optimal life. Through NRT, Jacob was able to eliminate all medications. He began his freshman year in high school and was able to self-regulate. Although we still had an IEP, it was just there for a backup. Jacob graduated and went on to a tech school studying early childhood education and lived on campus by himself two hours away while enjoying his independence. He is now living at home and doing an internship at We Rock the Spectrum, a kids' gym in Roswell, Georgia, designed to support kids of all abilities.

Jacob is currently juggling a hectic schedule. He's engaged in multiple activities, including playing and working with the kids as he completes this semester, assisting the owner in capturing videos and photos for promotional content on social media and for events, holding a part-time position at the local McDonald's, and embarking on his journey in Driver's Ed after recently obtaining his learner's permit. Jacob's superpower is his happy-go-lucky spirit. He is very agreeable. When asked to complete a task, if he is interrupted or reminded to do something, he does so with a happy heart. He can often be found waving his very long arms (he's 6'1") outside in the backyard, barefoot, and quoting YouTube videos. His favorite thing to do is take a scene in a movie and create a 'parody' of it by splicing in clips from other movies to fit the soundtrack of the selected scene. He can be found on his YouTube channel as Jacob DeWard, where he has over 360 videos and close to 1000 subscribers! I'm so amazed at the way his brain thinks.

One of Jacob's favorite things to do each year is to host the Camp DeWard Games. These are creative games that Jacob designs with a theme. He puts us into teams, and we work together to understand what he wants us to do. It has been so fun to see his creativity come to life each year! He even has a special recording at the beginning of the games with the national anthem that he rewrites parts of to fit the theme. Again, how his brain comes up with it all just blows us away. We enjoy watching his growing confidence and how proud he is to see us play the games he designed. I can only imagine decades from now still holding these Camp DeWard Games. It is such a wonderful way to be together as a family and support Jacob's creativity.

I asked him the other day how he would explain to someone what it's like to have autism. Without skipping a beat, he replied, "Well, it's like ping pong… except there are lots of paddles hitting the balls, and it's in an enclosed room with lots of walls, and the balls keep ricocheting off all the walls." Those who are close to Jacob at home and work can see this played out in real time. He seems to be everywhere and nowhere all at the same time. As frustrating as it can be for those around him, I can't imagine how that feels inside his head. I believe Jacob has a very bright future ahead of him. As is with all people with special needs, they are truly superheroes. They have to work so much harder to do the basic things so many of us take for granted, in the body or the brain. It's an honor and privilege to be a mom to all four of my amazing children and so blessed to parent these two superheroes that teach their world so much every day.

Find out more about Nicole DeWard here:

> www.shinehw.com
> www.rise-coffeetea.com
> LinkedIn: https://www.linkedin.com/in/nicoledeward/

STORY 10:
Liz Gabor

Mom and Advocate
Favorite Superhero: My son, Jeremy, and Spider-Man

While living on the Upper East Side of Manhattan, my husband and I were blissed and blessed to welcome our first son, Jeremy Frank, into the world on June 19th, 1998. Little did we know that our superhero in the making would be our greatest life teacher.

Very soon after Jeremy was born, I knew he was different. He was difficult to soothe and did not nurse well even though I was committed to nursing for at least one year. He seemed to have boundless energy and, at a very early age, was standing and bouncing on his little strong legs while we tried to hold him. He started walking, or rather running, before he turned nine months old. His bright, blue eyes (inherited from his namesake great grandpa Frank) were full of wonder and insatiable curiosity. Even then, I had a sense that we were embarking on a journey of uncharted territory.

When Jeremy was an infant, the local 'mommy and me' gatherings were being held in nearby restaurants on the Upper East Side. My first one was at a place called Hi-Life (no pun intended). Bar by night, and by day, it was a Iocal lunch gathering spot for moms and their infants ages 3 to 6 months. I figured I should check it out. At my first (and last) gathering, we were all seated in a circle and most of the babies were either being nursed or sleeping. However, my superhero wanted out! He cried, refused to nurse, and basically declared, "Let's get out of here!" Never one to give up, we tried a different mom and baby group held at a mom's apartment. The scene was similar to our Hi-Life experience. In both cases, the moms looked at me like I was disturbing the peace. Even though they didn't say it, their expressions said, "It's probably best if you take your adorable little superhero somewhere else." Next, we tried stroller walks where moms would walk New York city streets in order to get their babies to sleep. These walks also enabled the moms to hang out and have lunch for about 3 hours. My infant superhero napped for about an hour a day. In addition, he was a tiny Harry Houdini and could escape the chains of his stroller in under 30 seconds, making stroller walks a safety hazard in NYC. Thank goodness for the invention of the Baby Bjorn carrier. The contraption allowed my curious, energetic, little superhero to see everything while strapped to my chest (or my hubby's).

Although I have a psychology degree and a master's degree in social work, I had not extensively studied early childhood development. However, I did know that I was not going to put my 2 year old superhero through an interview process in New York City for preschool admission. My husband and I decided to relocate to a suburb in Westchester, New York and Jeremy began preschool around 2 ½ years old. He was halfway through his first year of preschool when we were called into school and informed that the teachers were concerned about Jeremy's attention and his ferocious appetite for exploring his environment. They said he needed to touch everything, had trouble staying seated, and had a lot of difficulty if the routine or structure of the day was changed in any way. Nevertheless, they noted that he consistently followed instructions, a trait that had always surprised teachers despite their initial assumption that he might be easily distracted. Still, their concerns persisted. Naturally, we decided to consult a doctor, and after just a few minutes of meeting both us and Jeremy, the doctor diagnosed him with ADHD (Attention-deficit/hyperactivity disorder). He also demonstrated characteristics consistent with autism like limited social interactions and hypersensitivity to noise and textures.

He received a lot of support as we navigated different schools from kindergarten through 8th grade. My background in social work also helped me navigate the school system and social services to get him the resources and services he needed and deserved. In addition, he found a safe haven in a small high school where his gifts were appreciated. He continued to learn and grow through his unique way of seeing and exploring the world. He actually declared where he would go to college after attending a summer film program at Champlain College in Vermont. Even though I suggested other college options, he eventually graduated with a broadcasting degree from Champlain.

Navigating social situations with Jeremy has often been a journey filled with understanding and advocacy. Some friends couldn't comprehend his unquenchable curiosity, his penchant for exploring every nook and cranny thoroughly, and a few offered unsolicited parenting advice about setting boundaries and manners. In response, I defended his innate curiosity, making it clear that if he wasn't accepted for who he is, it would be our last visit.

The social aspect of Jeremy's life has posed challenges, as he's struggled with reading social cues and engaging in small talk. Yet, when a topic piques his interest and aligns with someone else's, be prepared for a profound and expansive conversation. Ironically, small talk has never been my forte either. I battled social anxiety for years, often wishing to disappear when I felt my contributions weren't clever enough. I would slip into the shadows whenever possible, seeking refuge from the spotlight.

For my superhero, Jeremy, he had no choice but to show up as he was and never tried to be anything other than himself. As my greatest teacher, Jeremy has taught me the importance of not wavering from your truth, your authentic self. If we're open-minded and honest with ourselves, this truth is really refreshing. We are all just human with gifts and imperfections.

Jeremy has consistently amazed us with his talents. He's an exceptionally gifted singer, astonishingly organized, which might not be the norm for someone of his incredible nature, and he possesses a heart of gold. His unwavering love for humanity continues to inspire me. His heart overflows with pure love, and I couldn't be prouder of that, among all his other qualities. I hope that he finds opportunities to embrace his genuine spirit and acknowledge the worth of his talents. He's genuinely brilliant and everyone, including him, should be acknowledged, listened to, and cherished.

When I asked Jeremy who his favorite superhero is, he replied, "Spider-man," because he's a regular dude, relatable, not super rich, and he has problems just like the rest of us.

Find out more about Elizabeth Gabor here:

www.LizGabor.com

STORY 11:
Dr. Daniel Gary

Scientist and Autistic Adult
Favorite Superhero: Dr. Temple Grandin

I'm sorry I didn't understand you. I'm sorry that I ask too many questions. Finally, I'm sorry for who I am. I'm constantly masking who I am and then apologizing for being myself. This is what my life with autism looks like. Sensory overload, anxiety, and social difficulties can be unbearable. Despite these challenges, those with autism can be given unique gifts. Many people on the spectrum have a special interest they excel at and mine is chemistry. I'm going to tell you a story, not a story about a comic book superhero but a story about a boy who had a dream.

I'm fortunate to have a loving and supportive family, but my life has been full of challenges. Before I was born, my father was diagnosed with cancer. When I was 2, my father died, leaving behind a young mother with medical debt and a son. As a child, I had trouble speaking and was afraid. I didn't know my father but losing him had affected me in ways that I only now understand. I was terrified of losing my mother and would often cling to her. In pre-school, I was very quiet and didn't play with other children. There was hope that I would become more social when I started elementary school, but this was not the case.

Changes in routine have always been hard for me and kindergarten was not an exception. In addition to dealing with a dramatic change in my environment, my teacher abused me both emotionally and physically. I was even excluded from playtime sessions with other children. My teacher told my mother that I had a very low IQ. There were doubts about my long-term prospects. I was taken out of mainstream classes and enrolled in special education. Despite this, my mother's goal in every IEP meeting remained the same, and that was college. My mother saw something in me that many didn't. Although my mother never gave up, by the time I started third grade, I remained socially reserved, afraid, and anxious. I could barely read or perform basic arithmetic. I was then diagnosed with high-functioning autism. My future did not look promising and there were concerns about my ability to ever become independent, but all of that changed.

To say that my 3rd-grade teacher changed my life would be an understatement. Her support along with the support of my family made me realize that learning is fun. I started to love learning, and even my social skills started to improve. One school subject stood above the rest for me and that was science. By the end of third grade, I had dreams of becoming a scientist. At the end of the 5th grade, I was reading beyond an 8th-grade reading level and excelled in sciences but remained behind in math. Despite my academic struggles, it became clear that I was gifted as I could learn and retain enormous quantities of information on subjects that fascinated me.

The start of middle school was another change and, as expected, it was difficult. This change was even more complicated when a hurricane devastated my hometown of Sulphur, Louisiana. New friends I had just met moved away after losing their homes. My anxiety was bad. I felt alone and afraid, but I didn't give up. By the end of middle school, I was caught up and even ahead of my peers in mainstream courses. My dream of becoming a scientist now looked possible.

High School wasn't easy for me, and my anxiety got worse. I also began to realize how different I was from my peers. My outbursts became more severe and frequent. I was assigned a teacher's aid to help me cope. Autism can be complicated and one area that is often overlooked is its effect on motor skills. Between my anxiety and impaired motor function, learning how to drive was very difficult. Eventually, I would learn to drive and get my license but not until my late 20s. I would love to say these challenges never got me down but that would be a lie. I just wanted to be like everyone else. Despite these challenges, I kept pursuing my dream of science. When I discovered my passion for chemistry, I decided that I wanted to pursue my Ph.D. and become a research chemist. As someone who wanted to be a scientist, I knew that excellence in school was important. Furthermore, my sense of being different contributed to my feelings of insecurity, leading me to strive for academic excellence to compensate for what I believed were personal shortcomings. I studied for hours each day and became obsessed with grades. I ended up graduating with a 4.0 GPA. This intense studying would continue in college.

My undergraduate years as a chemistry student at McNeese State University were difficult, but I started to make improvements in my social skills. I made friends and have memories that I will cherish forever. I also noticed a dramatic improvement in my ability to handle my anxiety. I learned the power of friendships and in the end, I graduated summa cum laude and then pursued my Ph.D. in chemistry at Louisiana State University.

My transition into graduate school was not smooth, but I found my niche. I found a group where I felt accepted. My Ph.D. advisor was incredibly supportive and understood my challenges. In addition to going through a Ph.D. program, I continued to deal with crippling anxiety and financial hardship. I didn't have a vehicle and was in the process of still learning to drive. I walked over a mile to and from my lab each day. The global pandemic in 2020 significantly impacted my experience as a Ph.D. student. In addition to the pandemic disrupting my Ph.D. studies, my hometown was ravaged by the most powerful hurricane ever to strike Louisiana. Most people lost everything including close family members. Later that same year, a close friend of mine passed away. I'm not exactly an optimist and I wanted to give up, but I kept fighting and I graduated with several published papers and a pending patent. My dissertation was dedicated to my family and to those with disabilities who fight every day.

After my Ph.D., I started working in the chemical industry. I switched jobs after a year to find a place where I felt safe, accepted, and appreciated for who I am. I now work as a product development chemist for a coatings company. My work involves product modification and coatings innovation. My career in science has allowed me to utilize my unique gifts. I think in terms of numbers and pictures and can even visualize interactions occurring at a molecular level. These unique gifts combined with my ability to research and learn new topics rapidly have helped me tremendously as a chemist.

My dream of becoming a scientist came true, but I now have another dream. One day, I hope I wake up without fear. I want to live in a world where all my unique features are accepted. I dream that one day parents will be told by medical professionals and teachers that their autistic child is capable and has value. One day, I hope that public spaces, schools, and employers will be more accommodating and value unique gifts. I want to live in a society where being different isn't a hardship. Autistic people have a lot to offer to the world. We just need understanding, patience, and love. If you or someone you love has autism, remember my story. You aren't alone in this battle and in the wise words of Dr. Temple Grandin, you are "different not less."

Find out more about Dr. Daniel Gary here:

LinkedIn: https://www.linkedin.com/in/
daniel-gary-773aaa180/

STORY 12:
Dr. Emile Gouws

Autistic Adult, Educator, Researcher, Advocate
Favorite Superhero: Charlotte V. McClain-Nhlapo
(Global Disability Advisor to the World Bank Group) and Rassie
Erasmus (South African rugby union coach and former player)

At 4 years old, my teacher at pre-primary school noticed that my behavior was impaired and that I experienced challenges in language and communication, social interaction, flexibility in thinking, and sensory perception. My parents faced a challenging period as suspicions of a potential Autism Spectrum Disorder (ASD) diagnosis emerged. The school principal referred my parents to the local university where therapists did an in-depth evaluation. A multidisciplinary team observed my actions and asked my parents many questions about my behavior including social play, interest in other people, attention, and motor development. When I was 4 ½ years old, additional information was gathered about my intellectual functioning and adaptive behavior. My parents completed more screening questionnaires and interviews, but it was difficult for them to answer the questions because I was their first child, and they didn't have a frame of reference. Many tests, evaluations, and assessments rely heavily on auditory processing and verbal language, but I made no eye contact with the therapist. It was strange for my mom to see how my behavior changed in the presence of the therapist (a stranger). I was shy, withdrawn, and did not want to interact. During the evaluation, I froze and my speech was delayed. It took my mom years to realize that a change in environment affected my behavior significantly. If I visited unfamiliar places, I experienced complex processing problems and could not respond to verbal questions. After countless evaluations, doctors, psychologists, and therapists, there was some discussion about whether I should be institutionalized. My mother, however, decided to make a U-turn. My parents decided to seek private therapy from a multidisciplinary team, enroll me in mainstream schools, and expose me to an active lifestyle. The courage my Mom showed that day has stayed with me for many years.

I received therapy from a private team appointed by my parents, which included activities to enhance my memory and motor skills. These activities involved word and sound association, reading sentences from stories, and visual memory sequencing. Coaches assisted me with various leisure activities like ball play, swimming, pottery classes, tennis, and chess, contributing to my self-confidence. I also received occupational, speech, and psychological therapy, which improved my perceptual development. Despite making progress, certain challenges in numerical and writing abilities persisted, raising concerns about mainstream school placement. However, my parents decided to enroll me in a prominent mainstream school with 800 students, informing teachers about my ASD diagnosis. The large class size and unfamiliarity with classmates initially overwhelmed me. To cope, my mother and I worked through an Aquinas educational program at home, focusing on visual and auditory stimulation. Academically, my pace remained a challenge, and incomplete assignments were noted by the teacher. Despite these challenges, my parents prioritized affording me the same educational opportunities as neurotypical children.

In Grade 4, I started reading English rugby books, nurturing my special interest and expanding my English vocabulary. This newfound reading habit not only improved my academic performance in English as a first additional language but also played a pivotal role in my journey toward verbal communication in later years. My general knowledge blossomed, and I relished sharing insights with my parents while effortlessly recalling various facts. However, communication skills remained a challenge. Academic struggles began in Grade 4 as the pace quickened, with teachers unable to provide the extra support I needed during tests. Mainstream schooling didn't allow for extended exam time. I often felt rushed during tests, leading to penalties for incomplete work. Yet, occasional sparks of hope arose during exams when I tapped into my long-term memory. I discovered that visualizing information helped my brain process it faster, though this advantage didn't always translate into speedy test completion. I struggled to condense extensive knowledge into concise responses, a skill I was determined to eventually master.

From Grade 5 to 7, I felt overwhelmed with activities and struggled to focus due to overstimulation both at home and in the classroom. My attention span was fragmented, affecting my performance and leading to declining grades. To manage the workload, my mother created a helpful schedule, providing evaluation sheets for projects and meticulously organizing my assignments. This routine brought emotional security and improved problem-solving skills in a structured environment. Despite having applied for remedial placement since Grade 1, it was only in Grade 6 that we sought an education psychologist's evaluation due to bullying and academic challenges. The psychologist recommended a remedial school for high school, citing my Asperger's syndrome and emotional well-being as factors, even though my test scores didn't meet the criteria.

During this time, my coping mechanism involved increased hand gestures, which I used to unwind and feel more relaxed, especially in social situations. I became aware of being a target for bullying but struggled to stand up for myself or report incidents. Grade 6 marked a critical point in my education, prompting my mother to seek professional evaluation and recommendations for high school placement, ultimately leading to the psychologist's suggestion of a remedial school due to my emotional needs and ASD (then called Asperger's syndrome in my case).

For high school, I attended a school (MBS) for students who experience barriers to learning and development. The school was originally established for students with severe disabilities such as spina bifida, paraplegia, muscular dystrophy, and cerebral palsy. There are currently about 900 students total in grades 1-12 with approximately 400 of those students in high school. I believe I was the only student with ASD. Even though MBS was a remedial school, the content and volume of coursework were similar to mainstream schools. I still needed to put in the effort to receive good marks even with academic support. My mom continued to spend the afternoons assisting me with my academic work. On my first day at MBS, my confidence level increased, especially when I stepped into Miss Alicia's classroom (English register class). I noticed the class environment was smaller and one-on-one attention was provided. A huge weight seemed to lift from my shoulders. No longer was I overwhelmed with sensory stimuli. I could even focus and see the faces of my classmates. Some students even complimented my knowledge and long-term memory. For the first time in my life, I was acknowledged for my abilities.

In South Africa, upper secondary school, also known as further education and training (FET), lasts through grade 12 and offers educational and vocational training for careers such as Tourism, Office Administration, and Hospitality. As I progressed to FET, my self-confidence continued to improve. I received immediate feedback concerning my academic performance and thrived in MBS. I even learned to do my homework independently. My dedication and hard work paid off and I was one of the top five achievers in my grade. My academic success drove me to excellence and the hope for university studies. All students wanting to study at a South African university must obtain a university exemption to be admitted into tertiary studies.

And then the long wait began for the results…

On the day of the results, there was electric-like energy in our house. We got into the car and went to the nearest shop to buy a newspaper. With excitement and anticipation, I searched for my name in the newspaper. I knew there was a possibility of two distinctions. I achieved one distinction in Life Orientation but for Tourism, I achieved 79%. The next morning, we went to school and one of my teachers gave me a form to complete to request that my Tourism paper be remarked. We went to the Department of Education, but I did not obtain the Tourism distinction after the re-mark. I was, however, very happy and grateful about my overall average of 70.2% and I obtained my university exemption.

Not only did Dr. Emile Gouws attend university, but he also received a master's and PhD in Education from the University of Pretoria. Dr. Gouws is an active autism self-advocate and is currently the Vice Chairman of the Board of Autism South Africa, a Member of the Commonwealth Disability Forum, and newly elected President of the

Board of Directors at the International Council for Development and Learning (ICDL).

Find out more about Dr. Emile Gouws here:

LinkedIn: https://www.linkedin.com/in/ emile-gouws-610449116/

STORY 13:
Maximus Jarl

Autistic Adult, Student, Advocate
Favorite Superhero: Aquaman

My name is Maximus Jarl. At the time of writing this, I am 21 years old, and I live in Pleasantville, New York. I am in my final semester at Landmark College, a four-year institution in Vermont that is built specifically for those with learning differences such as autism, ADHD, or dyslexia.

Both on and off campus, I am an active member of the college community. Since arriving at Landmark in the fall of 2019, I have been a member of the college soccer team, though I have also tried my hand at basketball and baseball. Additionally, since the fall of 2022, I have been a part of the Campus Activities Board, the organization that plans and carries out recreational events and parties on campus. Starting in the spring of 2023, I began working at Landmark's Center for Diversity and Inclusion, which aims to 'promote meaningful learning and dialogue around issues of diversity, inclusion, and social justice through educational programming and advocacy'.

I have a multitude of interests that I partake in when I'm not involved in college activities. I have a genuine love for animals and enjoy spending time with my cat and two dogs at home. I also really love going out for walks and exploring different places, though this is difficult for me because I live in a suburban area and am unable to drive. Most of all, though, I am a big fan of sports, especially soccer, and I watch games whenever possible. Sometimes, I'll even take the hour-long train ride to New York City and spend the day at my favorite sports pub, McHale's Bar and Grill on 51st Street, where there are live matches every weekend, great food, and lovely staff.

What challenges have you faced living with ASD?

Over the years, I have faced some challenges living with autism. I received my autism diagnosis around the age of three. At the time, I did not know what autism was, and it would be several years later before I first even heard of the word. Around kindergarten, I was diagnosed with Tourette syndrome, which I had referred to as 'silly hiccups' until first grade when I learned the name of my condition. For the rest of elementary school, I would give a presentation each year to my class on Tourette syndrome. However, throughout middle school, I would often get made fun of or told to 'stop' having tics by fellow students, which irritated me to no end.

In high school, as people in my grade started becoming more aware of what Tourette syndrome was, they stopped giving me a hard time for my tics. However, because my reputation as the 'autistic kid' had been cemented so long ago, I was still the target of abuse from classmates. I have always been a non-confrontational person, avoiding conflict with others and hoping to get along well with everyone. However, when I was mistreated in school, I would often vent my frustration by getting back at those who insulted me, usually by insulting them back, which would lead to me getting in trouble while the other party would often not get punished. While I now recognize that this manner of retaliation was unhealthy and inappropriate, I was still deeply frustrated that the school's administration would seemingly keep me under a microscope while not doing anything about those who started the problems.

This pattern would continue, and after the end of a tumultuous junior year, my mother opted to pull me out of the Byram Hills district where I had spent all my school years. Though I was originally hesitant because there was only one more year, I eventually came around to accept the decision, hoping that it would lead to a better high school experience for my final year. My mother and I took tours of Mahopac High School before settling on the nearby Briarcliff High School, where I would spend my senior year. Though it was difficult to make friends in a completely new environment, the new students were all very accepting of me and I was not bullied. The year came and went, and soon enough, it was time for a very emotional graduation ceremony.

The college application process went rather smoothly. By the end of 2018, I had taken campus tours of the nearby Manhattanville College and Iona University as well as the relatively distant Mitchell College. However, I ultimately settled for Landmark College in southern Vermont, about a three-hour drive from my Pleasantville home. This college was designed specifically for those with learning disabilities, and many students are autistic as well. The faculty and staff are all very open and accepting of all, leading to an inclusive and welcoming learning environment. Although at times, I continue to struggle socially, I have found myself thriving academically, even having been accepted into multiple honor societies for my academic performance. I will be graduating from Landmark College in December 2023.

I have many hopes and dreams for the future, but my biggest aspiration is to get a decent job, leave home, and get a place of my own. In terms of occupation, I envision myself going into accounting, statistics, or another field that involves math and numbers as that is my strong suit.

I have never considered myself the materialistic type, so I do not care much about having an expensive home or any of the associated luxuries. Instead, I would be very happy just to have a nice apartment in a major city. Being unable to drive, I much prefer big cities since many necessities such as grocery stores and pharmacies are within walking distance and public transportation is readily available. Possible cities I could see myself living in are New York City, my father's childhood hometown of Karlstad, Sweden, or Berlin, Germany. I had the opportunity to study abroad in Berlin for three weeks and felt a sense of bliss that I had never felt before.

The biggest hope I have, regardless of where I end up living, is to be part of something larger than myself, as I have been at Landmark College. This could be anything from a recreational sports team, to the apartment community where I live, to a place such as a restaurant or bar that I regularly frequent. I have always thrived in communities and have never really done well on my own.

Who is my favorite superhero? Growing up, I was never really into superheroes or any sort of comic books or movies. However, if I had to pick one well-known superhero as my favorite, I would choose Aquaman, because of his connection to the ocean. The ocean has always been a source of fascination for me, and when I was younger not only did I love swimming, but I would love going to the aquarium and watching all the fish, something I still do when I get the chance.

> **Find out more about Maximus Jarl here:**
>
> LinkedIn: https://www.linkedin.com/in/
> maximus-jarl-04b318215
> Facebook: facebook.com/max.jarl.73
> Instagram: instagram.com/maxjarl

STORY 14:
Courtney Kaplan

Mom, Advocate

Favorite Superhero: My daughter

Do you remember waking up early Saturday morning to catch the cartoon mashup on the local TV channels? I spent a few of those early years watching the gray-white, two-tone tele until color made its way to the mainstream. Whether you were watching them in color or not, your favorite 'Superheroes' inspired strength and possibilities. As I have experienced life and all its glory, my definition of heroism has not changed. Today, I share with you a real-life 'Superhero', no cape or overly restrictive glossy leggings. She is my amazing daughter, Gabby 'Sweetest' Sigler.

From the very beginning, Gabby came into this world a quiet, calm, and loving soul. Being the youngest of five children, Gabby brought such a sense of peace and tranquility to the chaos cloud that hovered over our lives. She quickly nabbed the nickname, 'Sweetest,' causing certain jealousy amongst the natives.

Gabby progressed through the typical child development milestones. At a year old, however, we noticed Gabby was different. Her ability to babble and create speech was almost nonexistent. She would point, grunt, and drone when she needed something or someone. We sought the expertise of many, many pediatric specialists. With the consensus pointing to a choice versus an ability issue, the diagnosis remained a mystery. I had one of her pediatricians tell me she is non-verbal because she is the youngest child surrounded by siblings who are speaking for her, essentially, she was lazy. Needless to say, that was the last time we saw that doctor.

At three years old, Gabby began her journey with Early Intervention, a state-funded educational program that provides children with different abilities with supportive and adaptive education. Part of the program included an audiologist, occupational, physical, and speech therapy, as well as a developmentally appropriate classroom curriculum. It was determined by the professional consensus that Gabby was Low Functioning on the Spectrum Scale. These were words to describe autism at the time. As devastating as hearing such a label hurled at my baby was, there was also some relief. Finally, we had an idea of what her abilities were and how we can best support her journey.

Watching her develop into the individual she is has been one of my greatest gifts. Through all her challenges with communication, learning social awareness, and finding herself in silence, Gabby is a bright light. Gabby is kind, gentle, caring, tolerant, patient, and forgiving, the epitome of love as defined in the Bible in 1 Corinthians 13:4-8.

Gabby's presence is felt and celebrated in every school, every classroom, and every supportive program. It never fails. At any given time, at least two of my children attended the same school at the same time over the years. During high school, for one year, four of them attended the same school at the same time. On the rare occasion, I had to pick Gabby up from school early, the walk through the hallway was more like a red carpet event. Everyone, students and teachers, would acknowledge her presence with a huge smile, hugs, and a jazz-hands wave. Her smile could be seen from the moon along with her puffy cheeks, teeth-filled grin, and frown-curved slits where her eyes used to be. A hug from Gabby is a precious moment with the Prince of Peace, a glimpse into the light on the other side.

One early morning, Gabby's father and I woke to a loud slam that rocked the walls. I darted out of bed, and down a flight of stairs onto the landing. Slumped over at the bottom of the stairs is my seven-year-old, Gabby. Convulsing, thrashing, and barely breathing. From my medical training, I immediately laid her flat, rolled her on her side, and supported her precious little head. One minute seemed like hours. When she came to, she was disoriented and limp, her eyes were bloodshot, and she began to dry heave. This was our first taste of a life-long journey of epilepsy. My sweet Gabby.

Gabby's favorite book was, 'The Wheels on the Bus'. We would read that book, sing that book, and sleep with that book. It was our anthem. It was this book that encouraged her to verbally communicate by making more deliberate sounds and echoing words to the best of her ability. One day, Gabby was lying in bed, looking at her book, enjoying the peace of a new day. In the distance, I heard a faint tune coming from Gabby's room. I slowly made my way through the hallway, careful not to disturb the miracle in play. As I entered the threshold, I began to cry. Tears poured down my face, making no sound, mindful not to disturb the awakening before me. This was the first time I ever heard her beautiful voice. That is a day I will never forget as long as I live.

Gabby was well known for bringing non-customary items to school with her. In true Gabby fashion, she would leave the house with at least two kitchen utensils; a turkey baster, a neatly trimmed pastry brush, and my kitchen scrub brush. These are non-negotiable for any type of travel. She also enjoyed naked Barbie dolls, sometimes they were missing a limb or two, possibly headless, but usually intact with a couple of random bite marks. Barbie enjoyed the frequent dips in the bathtub. There were at least three opportunities a day.

Gabby loves the water, any water, pools, tubs, sinks. I can't tell you how many bottles of shampoo and conditioner, body wash, hand soap, and dish soap, brand new, were wasted down the sink. She was fascinated with the large bubbles that formed in the bottom of the upside-down bottles as they made their way down my sink. Shaving cream, baby powder, and lotion were not immune either. Panty liners stuck to the floor in a complex pattern, toothpaste finger art, and liquid foundation created murals only a mother could love. I remember the day before school pictures, Gabby chose to give herself a little haircut. Her hair is very curly. The bangs and the top of her head usually got the worst of it. This time, she found the clippers. We went to school with a landing strip running down the length of her crown. All I could do was laugh. Gabby was always up for a good laugh.

Gabby enjoyed playing by herself most of the time. As long as she had a tablet and one of her brushes, you wouldn't hear a peep. One of her favorite things to do is to eat. Food became a sensory soother around the age of 8. She would eat for stimulation, not hunger. Gabby began to gain weight. By the age of 11, she was about fifty pounds overweight. We had to fasten the refrigerator with a bike lock and hide the pantry items in the hope that she wouldn't eat herself to death. She continues to struggle with her feeding habits.

Just on the other side of pain is purpose. On the other side of darkness is light. When you're down, up greets your gaze. Healing is on the other side where grief meets gratitude. Gabby has the rest of her life to live in a world designed for the 'normal' and 'abled'. Gabby gets to show the world that the lives of people with different abilities hold just as much value and privilege as all the other people making the best of their journey. Doing all things through the power of love is a beautiful thing, and Gabby leads the way.

I believe there are two universal languages: unconditional love and music. Gabby has mastered the art of both. Communicating through love and music transcends the stereotypical barriers of what 'normal' is. 'Not' normal or 'dis' abled are two words that no longer belong in a 'Me too' society. Each individual comes with their own gifts, treasures that are uniquely theirs, gifts to share, and gifts to receive. Gabby is one of my greatest gifts. Gabby's superpower is and always has been, the sweetest!

You can learn more about Courtney Kaplan here:

www.transplanthope.com
LinkedIn: www.linkedin.com/in/
courtney-kaplan-b59027bb
Facebook: facebook.com/courtney.kaplan.52/
Instagram: instagram.com/courtneybkaplan/

STORY 15:
Gina Kavali, Bryan and Lyric Gillenwaters

Parents, Advocates
Favorite Superhero: Our son Lyric

Hi, my name is Lyric. I am in middle school, and just like all my friends, I like to listen to music, play games, and watch YouTube. My mommy has a show on YouTube called "Life With the Spectrum," and you should subscribe because sometimes she lets me make videos with her. Don't forget to like and subscribe to my channel, "LyricalGamester." I love doing challenges like other YouTubers do. I hope one day, Mr. Beast follows my channel, or I get to meet him. My parents told me I was diagnosed with Autism when I was four years old. I don't remember that, but I do remember going to different therapies. My parents are always open with me about autism. To me, being autistic isn't a disadvantage, but rather a superpower without a cape, kind of like the Hulk. I see things differently, and that's not a bad thing. Some people may not understand me, so my parents try to help others understand people with differences. When I grow up, I want to be a radio engineer like my dad, get married, and have four kids. My wife can work, and I will stay at home. My mom is helping me learn how to treat girls, and she started this cool event in Atlanta called "Table Talk." The event helps teach young adults on the spectrum how to date, and sometimes I get to come and host some of the events. I know one day I will have the best girlfriend ever!

From your friend

– Lyric

As Lyric's parents, we are beyond proud of him. He continues to amaze us every day and always rises to the occasion. Let me give you a little backstory on Lyric. He was deprived of oxygen at birth and had difficulty breathing. When he finally took his first breath, he ripped a hole in his lung and was sent to the NICU (Neonatal intensive care unit). The nurses teased us that he was the biggest baby in the NICU because he was born full term. At one year old, we started noticing that he wasn't meeting certain developmental milestones and had high and low muscle tone. We started early intervention, but at that time, ASD was not diagnosed until a child was nearly four. Nowadays, it is diagnosed much earlier, allowing for early intervention to happen much sooner. We truly believe that early intervention is key, and Lyric wouldn't be doing as well today without it. As advocates for people with disabilities, we are happy to see that the state of autism is changing. Classrooms are becoming more inclusive, and companies are hiring a more diverse workforce, including individuals with various challenges and disabilities. It warms our hearts to see communities popping up across the country for our neurodiverse individuals. As our kids become young adults, they are living with aging parents, and we worry about their future. These communities are being built just in time to address those needs, providing opportunities for living independently and with gainful employment, and for the more profound, day programs where they can contribute to society through volunteering and spreading joy. If we ever won the lottery or came into riches, we would start building such a community here in Atlanta.

I remember taking Lyric to Washington DC for spring break and world autism day. He was obsessed with the Presidents at the time. We toured the White House, and even the Secret Service was impressed with Lyric's knowledge about all things Presidential. He was hoping and praying that the President would come down for a chat. Unfortunately, the President was away that day and they didn't get to meet one another. Sometimes we see Lyric become hyper-focused on things. One year, it was the Little Mermaid, the next it was the Presidents, and now, it's the Wu-Tang Clan. I know it may seem like we go from one extreme to the other, but most people on the spectrum are very black and white and don't pick up on that gray area that some of us do. We are always transparent with Lyric so that he is empowered to make good choices every day. As of now, Lyric is on track to finish school, drive a car, go to college, and find his own way.

If you were to ask my husband, Bryan, and me who our favorite superhero is, we would say, hands down, it is Lyric! He continues to teach us something new every day. His mind looks at the world and all the people in it differently. Just the other day, I was bothered by something for months, and I thought it was so important. I brought it up to Lyric, and the way he broke it down made me realize that it wasn't really important at all. You know the saying, "You meet one autistic person, you meet one autistic person." It's true that no two people on the spectrum are alike, but what is true is that the autistic brain looks at things differently. That's why Dr. Temple Grandin came up with the saying, "Different, not Less." It truly applies.

As parents, we often reinvent ourselves on this crazy journey called life. We arm ourselves with as much information as possible because it's essential that we're not only informed, but also prepared. I've spoken with many parents who have started non-profit groups, clubs, organizations, foundations and/or companies that only hire neurodiverse staff. There are so many amazing people out there being a force for good, and the potential for you and your children is endless! PS. If Lyric runs for President one day, you can expect Bryan and I to be knocking on your door for a vote.

Find out more about Lyric Gillenwaters here:

YouTube: LyricalGamester

Find out more about Gina Kavali here:

YouTube and Facebook: Life with the Spectrum
Gkasts.com
LinkedIn: https://www.linkedin.com/in/
gina-kavali-44550813/

STORY 16:
Becky Large

Mom, Founder, and Advocate
Favorite Superhero: Underdog

I have always been an autism mom since the birth of my first child. For the last decade, I became an advocate for people living with autism, this includes the person with autism, their parents, siblings, extended family, and caregivers.

It took until our oldest was 7 years old to get the diagnosis of Pervasive Developmental Disorder-Not Otherwise Specified (PDD NOS), Attention Deficit Hyperactivity Disorder (ADHD), and Autism (Aspergers). It was a challenging time knowing there were more services and support and wringing our hands trying to figure out where, how, and when we could access them. Like many on this journey, it was like pulling a thread that you just couldn't let go of to find providers and therapies while also seeking answers and meaningful support from the Child Support Team (a topic for another day or book).

Shame, anxiety, and isolation!, Don't get me started. With unaware family, friends, neighbors, teachers, community, and business owners, our world was shrinking. Everyday things could be a trigger and if a tantrum occurred shopping, grocery shopping, or going to a restaurant could be a nightmare. Participating in holiday family gatherings or neighborhood parties was ridiculously stressful. The judgment we faced was astonishing. Even people we love made my husband and I feel as though we were bad parents, urging us to discipline instead of nurture or encourage.

In 2012, we relocated from the Philly/Southern New Jersey area to Surfside Beach, South Carolina, near Myrtle Beach. We arrived at our new home on Easter Sunday. The importance of this date is not lost on us; we consider this our family's resurrection. I truly believe, if we hadn't moved, our family would not be intact today. It is easy to see how the divorce rate among autism parents is so high; life with autism is relentless and unpredictable. The more rigid our loved ones with autism can be, the more flexible we need to be as parents and caregivers.

Our sons were in 1st and 3rd grade at the time of the move. Our oldest was diagnosed with Autism (Aspergers) and ADHD and the youngest with ADHD and sensory processing disorder.

It was a HUGE move as you can imagine. We were in a totally new environment, going from a major metropolitan area in the Northeast to the Deep South and Bible Belt. No more, "Hey dude," and "Thanks." In South Carolina, we heard "Yes ma'am," "Yes sir," "Have a Blessed Day," and my personal favorite, "Bless Your Heart." If you are unaware, "Bless Your Heart" is a special Southern double entendre and can be used as an insult of the highest degree.

I do believe the move was good for our children, especially our oldest. Living in the South, where there is a relatively uniform set of social norms, can be an advantage for someone who tends to see the world in black-and-white terms. Having fewer social expectations during my son's formative years was a benefit.

It wasn't until sophomore year in high school that we learned his superpower. Unfortunately, it took him being overwhelmed with school, leading to depression and suicidal thoughts, for this very important realization to occur. I was told by a highly respected psychiatrist who specializes in autism to take away all stress and let him know his happiness and well-being were more important than school or getting a high school diploma. This was a huge gut punch for my husband and I. Both of us have college degrees and my husband is an attorney. We expected our children to go to college. We realized that our expectations were a big part of our son's crisis. This experience was very sobering and was an unexpected wake-up call for us as autism parents.

We knew his schedule had to be significantly altered. His case manager on the Child Study Team suggested that he pick a 'brain break' class, perhaps something in music. He chose guitar and that choice changed everything.

At his senior concert, he SLAYED it! We had no idea how talented he was until that performance, and I shed tears of joy as he played his heart out and the audience stood, screamed, and applauded him. A few years and several guitars later, he still plays. We hope and pray that he will find his path using this superpower, but as we've learned, it is HIS path. We must be patient, and supportive and know that everything takes longer than any of us want.

As a layperson with little or no connection to autism, we want you to know when you see a child in public having a tantrum or a meltdown, please know that this very well could be a family in distress. Do not judge or say anything condescending or rude. If you offer support, do not be upset if your kind offer is declined. Try to understand we are in panic mode and trying to figure out how to diffuse the situation. We have no idea how to incorporate anyone else into the scene. However, KNOW that your kindness will NEVER be forgotten.

This is why we don't want to leave the house. The disruption in routine, leaving the house, or even taking a different way to the store can trigger a meltdown. We just never know. It truly is easier to just stay home. But what good does that do anyone? As parents and advocates, we must teach our loved ones with autism that change is the only constant in life. It is an arduous task for all involved and requires baby steps and patience from all family members.

Don't forget the siblings. Imagine that the family plans to go to the movies or an attraction. The siblings are excited for an outing, everyone has been talking about it, prepping the person with autism. Then the day comes and, if you're lucky, you manage to get everyone into the car almost on time. If you're fortunate, you might get everyone into the movie or attraction. And if you're even luckier, your family members enjoy their time there. However, often, the person with autism cannot handle the situation or environment and is on the brink of or has a tantrum. ☹ Depending on the circumstance, this is when 1) the family splits up with one parent taking the person with autism away so the rest of the family can try to enjoy the outing or 2) the entire family must leave cutting the activity short. Imagine how much anxiety results from every step in this scenario.

A study conducted by the University of Wisconsin found mothers with children with autism have similar stress levels as combat soldiers. Work interruptions, food not being quite right, an irritating tag in his shirt, and generally not knowing what is in store—not just day-to-day, but minute-by-minute. Knowing this, please provide autism moms, dads, and families love, encouragement, smiles, and support. We are the underdogs. We're doing our best to be upbeat, organized, seemingly happy, and put together, when in reality we're walking on eggshells, foregoing self-care, trying to juggle everything, chauffeuring to school and different therapies, supporting the siblings and maybe even steal a few minutes to have some 'quality time' with our spouse or partner.

It is important that autism parents know that they are not alone. Autism can be isolating but with more awareness, acceptance, and support it doesn't have to be that way. Creating communities of understanding is my sole purpose in life. I wouldn't be doing this without my son and now it is much bigger than him.

Find out more about Becky Large here:

Champion Autism Network:
https://championautismnetwork.com/
Autism Travel Club: https://autismtravel.club/

STORY 17:
Bobby Latherton

Autistic Adult, Musician, Author
Favorite Superhero: my family, friends and musicians like
Adele and Celine Dion

Music affects everyone in one way or another. For me to understand
and express emotions, it is easier if I use music as the vessel. For
people with autism, processing emotions is difficult. One way that I
can express my emotions is when I am in a place where others understand me. That place is the Autism Matters group.

I first became interested in music as a young child. I loved songs
older than my time such as Celine Dion. I remember standing on
the dining room table in my nappy and singing "My Heart Will
Go On" to my Nana. I have older siblings who influenced me with
the music they listened to in the style of the 90's and 00's. I just remember a mic was always in my hand. Anywhere I went, the mic
went with me. My love for music just grew and grew. One of my
first emotional struggles happened when I was 4 and my Nana died
suddenly of cancer. Even though I was young, I knew music was a
way for me to escape. Music was also my escape when I struggled

with my sexuality and chose to be in bad relationships. I kept things to myself, but music changed everything for me. I could express my feelings and deal with my emotions. Music also kept me from wanting to harm myself; it protected my mental health. I want to spread the word that there's always a way forward; discovering your passion and focusing on it can be a lifeline.

For my 21st birthday, my sister, Zena, bought me singing lessons because she knew how much I enjoyed singing karaoke. To this day, it is the best present I have ever received. My own singing lessons, WOW! The night before my first singing lesson, I was at my Autism Matters social group and speaking to a member of my support staff. I was so excited to tell her all about the lessons, including that I was going to Teesside for the lessons. She shared with me that Teesside is where one of the Journey South brothers live. Journey South is an English singing duo, two brothers from Middlesbrough, North Yorkshire. I couldn't believe it. Maybe one of them would be teaching me? Surely not. They'll be big time now…

I was beyond excited on the first day of my new singing lessons. I was too excited for words and constantly thinking about who was going to be teaching me. Thoughts were running around my head as I was getting ready. My brother was kind enough to drop me off. From the outside, the place looked like a normal house. I wondered if I was in the right place. A guy named Carl then appeared at the door and welcomed me in. Introductions were made, but I could hardly pay attention as I took in the studio and looked around. It was incredible. I was in awe of the huge studio with guitars and pictures everywhere. Even though there were pictures of Journey South, I was still too shy to ask if it was them. Carl asked me to get ready and get on stage to sing a song. I was a bit nervous as I walked up to the mic. I took a deep breath and got myself together but before I could belt out the lyrics, I had to ask, "Are you Journey South by any chance?" When he replied, "Yes," I was amazed. It was Carl Pemberton from Journey South! I told him I wasn't singing in front of him (haha). My talent is more geared towards writing songs and not singing, even though I love singing, too.

We started looking at my love of songwriting and it flourished from there. Writing songs helps me process emotions. I have a lot of friends in my social group, Autism Matters, and one of those was Ziggy. When I heard of the death of my friend Ziggy, I felt all sorts of emotions. As I was walking one day and thinking of Ziggy, song verses started to form. I then worked with Carl to get those emotions out to form the tribute song. I wrote the lyrics, but the wonderful Carl Pemberton and Beth Miller (aka Beth Jackson) sang it.

As I mentioned previously, people with autism can struggle to express emotions and this can come out in other ways such as depression or outbursts. It was important to me to write the tribute song to express my own emotions but also honor Ziggy's memory. Although Ziggy is not with us, I believe he knows through the song how much we love him. I am inspired by many artists such as Celine Dion and Adele. It doesn't matter to me what era the music comes from; what matters is how I connect. I feel the emotions through the lyrics when I listen to both artists. Currently, I have written about 10 songs and they are only available on YouTube. I have received feedback and many have shared that they find the song I wrote for Ziggy emotive and a great tribute. People have said the song brought them to tears, especially those who knew Ziggy. If anyone would like to listen you can find it on YouTube, it's called "Missing You." I am working to offer "Missing You" through Spotify. I am so lucky to have worked with some great local singers.

I want to share my journey with autism to help others grasp the complexity of my thought patterns and the challenges many with autism encounter in society. Whether you describe me as 'with autism' or 'autistic,' I'm comfortable with either label. I've also written a book, "My World, In My Words," which gives insight into my experiences growing up with autism. Before gathering others' perspectives on the condition, I wanted the narrative to be purely mine, untouched by external influences. The book concludes with a screenplay revealing a whimsical love story, a window into my imagination. At 27, hailing from Middlesbrough, North Yorkshire, England, I'm ardently working towards amplifying awareness and providing support for others living with autism.

Find out more about Bobby Latherton here:

His book *My World, In My Words* is available at Waterstones in Middlesbrough, North Yorkshire (UK) or online at Amazon.

STORY 18:
Dr. Kerry Magro

Autistic Adult, Speaker, Author, Consultant, Advocate
Favorite Superhero: Autistic people everywhere

I'm Dr. Kerry Magro, and as you flip through my contribution here, you're about to journey alongside me. Consider this our shared superhero comic. A tale with fewer capes but filled with the highs and lows of my life on the autism spectrum.

What challenges have I faced living with autism spectrum disorder (ASD)? I was nonspeaking until I was 2 ½ years old. By the age of 4, the term "autism" became an indelible part of my story. Navigating social norms often felt like deciphering an alien language, and the sensory storms could be both overwhelming and disorienting. But these challenges, as daunting as they might seem, have sculpted me, pushing boundaries and opening doors to newfound strengths.

With my trusty pen, I've chronicled my journey and the tales of many others in the autism community across four books. From "Defining Autism from the Heart" to the raw emotions in "Autism and Falling in Love", the beacon of hope in "I Will Light It Up Blue!", to the collective chorus in "Autistics on Autism", they're testaments to our shared experiences.

My strengths included being able to find success in basketball and theater. One of my role models, another autistic self-advocate, is Dr. Temple Grandin. Dr. Grandin likes to say, "Interests and talents can turn into careers."

What do I wish the world knew or understood about ASD? When I stand in front of students or professionals, my aim isn't just to present but to peel back the layers of a world that's often overlooked. I dream of a place where ASD isn't a mere clinical term but is cherished for the diverse perspectives and creativity it brings. I also hope that more people understand that we also need to spotlight that autism is a spectrum and some will need constant care for their entire lives.

Overall, I hope we can also debunk the common stereotypes such as:

- Every autistic person is great at math,
- Every autistic person is a white male,
- Every autistic person has a photogenic memory,
- Every autistic person is a child (autism doesn't end at 18!),
- Every autistic person lacks empathy, and
- Every autistic person has savant syndrome (like "The Good Doctor" or "Rain Man")

I hope we also start to understand that advocacy isn't just about speaking up. It's about listening, understanding, and creating bridges of empathy. In my quest to be a voice for the community, I've come to realize that the most profound moments are those where someone else's experiences echo in our own hearts. It's about creating a world where every individual feels heard and seen.

I also want the world to know that romantic relationships may be possible for some on the spectrum. Like many other aspects of life, these relationships present their own set of challenges for those on the spectrum. The nuanced world of emotions, connections, and communications can sometimes feel like an intricate dance. And yet, like everyone else, many of us dream of love, of building a life with someone who understands and cherishes us. The dream of finding someone who sees beyond the spectrum and embraces the person beneath is universal.

What are my hopes and dreams? Beyond everything, my heart yearns for a world where every soul, irrespective of their place on the neurodiversity spectrum, feels valued and supported. A place where each of us can chase our dreams without the weight of misconceptions holding us back. It's this dream that fueled the birth of the nonprofit I founded called "KFM Making a Difference" – a beacon illuminating paths toward inclusive education and boundless opportunities. I've been able to give scholarships to autistic students for college along with other disability initiatives to support others in our community.

I have more dreams I hope that can come to fruition as well. I've had the opportunity to be an autism consultant on projects like "Love on the Spectrum U.S." and hope I can do similar projects like this in the future. One day I hope I can get married and be a father too. I've been able to reach many of my professional goals and hope my personal goals can be reached as well.

Moving forward, with every page turned, every speech given, and every story shared, my vision for the future grows brighter. I envision a society where acceptance isn't the exception but the norm. I envision a world where understanding autism goes beyond mere awareness and translates into tangible actions that make a difference. In this ever-evolving narrative, our community isn't just seeking understanding; we are crafting a world of endless possibilities. A world where every child, teen, and adult on the spectrum knows that their dreams are valid, their voices matter, and their futures have potential.

Together, let's continue this beautiful journey of discovery, understanding, and above all, unwavering hope. The tapestry of our shared experiences is rich, diverse, and endlessly inspiring. Let's embrace it with open hearts and continue to champion the cause of a world where every individual shines in their unique brilliance.

And ah, who's my favorite superhero? You might be thinking of caped crusaders or shield-wielding warriors. A part of me will always have a love for Iron Man and Captain America. Iron Man for using his brain to create incredible inventions and Captain America for never giving up. I know so many families who remind me of the latter. One quote I like to share in many of my talks is, "Autism doesn't come with an instruction guide. It sometimes comes with a family who will never give up." But in my eyes, my true favorite superheroes are found in everyday life. They're every individual on the spectrum, every person going after their dreams and striving for a better day for our autism community.

I like to say that autism can't define me and I define autism. As our society progresses with the concept of superheroes, I hope that both self-advocates and their supportive loved ones can step out into the world each day and shape their lives and journeys according to their own terms.

Find out more about Dr. Kerry Magro here:

https://kfmmakingadifference.org/
Facebook: Kerry's Autism Journey
Kerry is the author of several best-selling books including "Defining Autism From The Heart," "Autism and Falling in Love," "I Will Light It Up Blue," and "Autistics on Autism."

STORY 19:
Nicholas McMahill

Advocate, Community-Builder, and Podcast Host
Favorite Superhero: The people in my community are all heroes.

The turning point for me was when one of my teachers recognized that I displayed signs of autism. It was a pivotal moment that set me on a path of self-discovery and understanding. This compassionate teacher, with a keen eye and a heart full of empathy, saw beyond my struggles and recognized the potential within me. It's incredible how a single person's intervention can change the course of a life. This teacher's support opened the door to the resources and assistance I desperately needed.

Reflecting on my journey, I firmly believe that an earlier diagnosis could have spared me from many of the challenges I faced. Autism awareness and access to resources can significantly impact the lives of those on the spectrum. It's not just about identifying the condition; it's about ensuring that individuals receive the support and understanding they need to thrive. An earlier diagnosis might have led to a smoother educational journey and a more profound sense of self-acceptance.

As an autistic individual, I've come to understand the vital role advocacy plays in creating a more inclusive and accepting world. It's not enough to focus solely on personal growth; we must also strive to break down barriers for others. One area where I'm particularly passionate about advocacy is the interactions between first responders and individuals on the spectrum. It deeply concerns me when I see instances of misunderstandings or escalated situations involving autistic individuals and those tasked with maintaining public safety. My commitment to advocacy has led me to take action. I've initiated workshops and programs aimed at providing first responders with the knowledge and skills they need to interact effectively with neurodiverse individuals. It's my hope that these efforts will lead to a safer and more inclusive society where autistic individuals can live without unnecessary fear or miscommunication.

One of the most significant steps I've taken in my advocacy journey is the creation of my blog, "Nicholas's Journey." This platform allows me to share my experiences, challenges, and triumphs with the world. It's a space where I can be open and transparent about my life on the spectrum. Starting this blog wasn't easy; I had to take baby steps, gradually building my platform, and finding my voice. Through "Nicholas's Journey," I've connected with a community of readers who share their stories, offer support, and seek to better understand autism. It's a place where I've learned that opening up and sharing my experiences can inspire and educate others. The power of storytelling cannot be underestimated, and it has become a cornerstone of my advocacy efforts.

My journey has been significantly influenced by two mentors, Anthony and Joey, who have guided and supported me along the way. One mentor, in particular, Anthony, has played a crucial role in my life. Anthony has encouraged me to be transparent, confident, and unapologetically myself. He's been there to provide guidance, advice, and a helping hand whenever I've needed it. Perhaps one of the most significant impacts both Anthony and Joey have had on my life is their encouragement for me to pursue higher education. As an autistic individual, going to college can be daunting, but I'm determined to overcome these challenges. I've learned that with the right support system and the belief in oneself, anything is possible. My mentors' unwavering support has shown me the importance of mentors in helping us reach our full potential.

As I look toward the future, I have ambitious dreams and goals. I want to expand my reach and impact by potentially creating a podcast network that can further advocate for neurodiversity and inclusion. These dreams are a testament to my determination and my belief in the power of advocacy. While my dreams may seem grand, they are rooted in a desire to make a positive change in the world. I want to continue breaking down barriers, dispelling misconceptions about autism, and promoting understanding. Every step I take brings me closer to these goals, and I'm excited to see where this journey leads me.

My life as an autistic individual has been marked by challenges, triumphs, and a commitment to advocacy. While receiving a late diagnosis presented its own set of obstacles, it ultimately led me to a path of self-discovery and empowerment. Through advocacy, storytelling, and the support of mentors, I've been able to make a positive impact in the world. I hope that by sharing my journey, others will find inspiration and strength to embrace their neurodiversity. We all have our unique superpowers, and it's up to us to use them to create a more inclusive and understanding world. Autism is not a limitation but a different way of experiencing the world, and it's a part of who I am. Embracing neurodiversity is not just a personal journey; it's a collective effort to build a brighter and more inclusive future for all.

> **Find out more about Nicholas McMahill here:**
>
> Facebook: Nicholas's Journey

STORY 20:
Caryn Mittleman

Mom and Advocate
Favorite Superhero: The Livingston Parent Self-Help Support
Group (LPSHSG)

My son is incredible, and he happens to live with Autism Spectrum Disorder. He has many notable accomplishments and talents. For example, he built a computer and game room from the ground up; is proficient at using the computer, video games; and paintball, plays the guitar and has a melodious voice; is very handy with tools; is a 'jack of all trades;' likes to cook; and is a creative artist who can sketch well and take beautiful photographs that capture perfect moments.

My son also has work experience and gathered some important skills. He worked as a ride operator at Six Flags Great Adventure for over a year. He loved being an employee there and they loved him. He told me he is a performer and the job allowed him to be himself. He was given many awards by Six Flags for his excellent work ethic. His Support Coordinator wrote an article about his Six Flags success story for her agency's monthly bulletin. Thinking about my son working in a giant amusement park was way out of my comfort zone, but I listened and heard that it was within his comfort level.

We have been through a life-altering journey together that imparted us with a lot of wisdom. Through infancy and into adulthood, there were many challenges from socialization, school, family issues, friends, doctors, and the public. I was always researching ways to help my son. I ultimately learned the best way to help him was to communicate with him by being quiet, using active listening skills, and learning directly from him. I listened intently to his words when he spoke about his feelings and put my feelings aside. I was listening to understand, not to respond, and to meet his needs, not mine. Actively listening made a significant impact on our relationship.

My son was not born with a manual! I had to learn how to parent him in ways that would support his needs. I joined the Livingston Parent Self-Help Support Group (LPSHSG) in Livingston, NJ and became one of the group leaders. The parenting group helped me establish rules, consequences, and consistency for my son's complicated behaviors. The parenting group taught me to stop pleading with my son to change his unhealthy choices and let the rules and consequences do the talking instead. One day, my son told me, "Mom, I do not like your rules, but they make me feel like I have different choices!" My son's realization that he could make better choices with good behavior was a positive turning point in his life. I am extremely grateful for the superheroes at LPSHSG. Their unwavering support and guidance made us feel like we were never alone.

He is compassionate. His expression of concern for the suffering of others is truly genuine. He likes giving money to charities at the food store. He also has a great sense of humor and is always telling jokes. Once he removed a bush from our garden and threw down some mulch while I watched. I wanted to take pictures of the beautiful garden when he was done and he said, "Wait, Mom, at least put dirt on your hands so it looks like you helped!" There were laughs all around.

Over the years, I've searched for ways to connect and bond with my child, not his diagnosis. We made a deep-rooted connection by sharing music and baking brownies together. He loves sharing music, and who doesn't love brownies! I've always wished for my son to experience unconditional love, and I believed that creating these non-judgmental memories together would help him feel that way. I've also tried to demonstrate that I believe in him. When he was young, I'd write him an uplifting message, leaving it by his bedroom door on a post-it note, along with a sweet chocolate kiss attached. When my son was struggling, I printed a picture of a Hershey's Kiss outline. In the paper plume where the word "Kisses" appears, I wrote, "I believe in you!" and laminated the picture. He told me he slept with it under his pillow for many years. I'm glad that expressing my belief in my son provided him with the inner strength to keep pushing forward toward his goals. Despite facing numerous challenges, he has displayed remarkable perseverance and resilience.

I've taught my children about kindness, unconditional love, forgiveness, speaking with a kind tone, communicating, and helping others. They have implemented these qualities into their lives. I love the saying, "When given the choice between being right or kind, choose kind." I made a clock with this saying to remind me how I want to interact/act with others and not react, especially with my children. It makes me stop and choose my words and tone carefully before I speak. Throughout our journey, I had hoped that the message on the clock would serve as a source of inspiration for all of us. Now, it's my son who serves as a reminder of that quote.

The other phrase that I use frequently with my son is, "It is all good!" Positive reinforcement!

Recently, we had a 90th birthday party for my mom and my son was engaged and attentive during the entire party. After he left, he wasn't answering his cell phone. I was very concerned, but he eventually called me. We had such an honest and insightful discussion. He told me that even though he had a great time with our family, it was stressful for him, and he needed some time to be alone and decompress. I thanked him for sharing this vital information with me and realized it would help me communicate more effectively with him in the future. During our conversation, he helped me understand how he was feeling, and I was able to actively listen and put my opinions aside.

After 25 years of advocating for my son and learning from each other, I realized that he is one of my best friends! He is charismatic, kind, intelligent, and keeps moving the needle forward. On other days, it is more complex, but we continue to learn. Watching my son make positive strides in his life, such as renting an apartment, living with a caregiver, making plans for his future, searching for employment, and taking on more responsibility, makes my heart smile. My hopes and dreams for my son are for him to motivate others living with autism through his exceptional story. He is impressive and continues to defy the odds. I hope my son can live the best life he can, always feel the warmth of unconditional love and acceptance, be true to his extraordinary personality, be consistent at making good choices, and believe in himself.

Find out more about Caryn Mittleman here:

Website: ItIsAllGood.org

STORY 21:
Jamiel Owens

Dad, Advocate

Favorite Superhero: My son, Shayne

Imagine being in the beautiful waters of the Caribbean with your son. The water feels comfortably warm, so there's little need to gradually acclimate your body to its temperature. You see your 'Ausome' child staring deep into the beauty given to us by a divine power. He's gathering his energy and focusing on living in the moment but also teaching me simultaneously. Many who know 'evidence-based' research may refer to this as a 'hiccup' in the brain of an individual diagnosed with Autism, but as an 'Ausome' father, I soon realized that it was another life lesson my son Shayne was teaching me.

I remember floating near him in the beautiful water of "Isla Verde" Beach in Puerto Rico. It was a family trip that was long overdue and much needed for all of us. When I approached him, he was startled by my touch on his shoulder and said, "Hey Dad, I'm just meditating. I want to be alone!" His response was a shock and I had to fight hurt feelings. I respected his wish and gave him space, yet an inner urge prompted me to seek an alternative reaction. Returning to his space in the water, I asked him if he was ok. "Of course," he responded but his follow-up surprised me. He asked to be alone again. I became worried, as would other parents, but I also had a sense of relief and profound happiness. This request meant my son was thinking and feeling for himself as a man. For a moment, there was no pressure for me to bend time at my expense so that I could ensure his safety and security for the future. At that moment, I didn't care about the time I missed with Shayne because of countless court proceedings to establish my rights on paper when God divinely gave me the right to be his father. At that precise moment, I was absorbed in his world without realizing it. In the peace and beauty of the beach, I was seeing everything through his eyes, and most importantly his heart. I asked him if I could join him in his meditation and he allowed me. For five minutes, we gracefully floated with our eyes closed and airways open, experiencing pure bliss entering our lungs and into our souls. Given the trauma I experienced in my later youth, I've become deeply drawn to the enduring innocence my son, now 15, still possesses. I asked him, "Do you trust me?" and he responded, "Yes." I asked if I could help him support him floating in the water while he closed his eyes and meditated. He agreed! At that moment, I felt more at peace about everything in my past, present, and future than I ever felt before. I was 100% committed and in his world. I wasn't taking the stance of a worried parent, or teacher, but was broken down to simply 'being in the moment' with my son.

As special needs parents, we are typically too focused on interventions and miss out on the moments of enjoying life with our loved ones. Yes, we need to do what is immediately necessary to support our children. However, is it right to neglect our mental health in that process?

I was lost in a trance, rotating my body in a 360-degree motion as I maintained Shayne's body afloat in the same rotation. It was truly an out-of-body experience where we connected on a level of simplicity. It wasn't about me speaking about the importance of advocacy and why I started my platform, non-profit, or journey in this field. Nor, was it about the fathers raising children with special needs who were excited about connecting and looking to me for support and mentoring. In that singular moment of my life, it was about nothing, and the sensation was surreal.

I once mentored an autism father who called me frantically from New York. His son did not want to come inside and it was raining outside. This amazing father and I connected via social media, and we often talk about challenges we both face. I remember this conversation like it was yesterday because it left me with a profound thought. I remember saying, "Go out there with him! If your son wants to stand or sit in the rain, be right next to him and enjoy that moment. There is something there that he is trying to show you!" The brief pause following my words revealed to me that he had never sat in the rain with his son. I quickly reinforced his thoughts with the reminder to just be IN THE MOMENT! The father quickly responded with a semi-agreeable, "Okay" and proceeded to hang up and go outside with his son. The next day I received a text from him saying it was the most amazing time he had ever had with his son. They connected in a way that he had never experienced before. After some time, he suggested to his son that it was time to go in and his son simply said, "Okay, Daddy."

As you read the stories in this book shared by extraordinary individuals from diverse backgrounds and experiences, I want to highlight two insights I hope you take away from my story. First, I invite you to remember that our 'Ausome' children will be great! They are looking at the world with nothing but love, empathy, and compassion. There is the quote, "If you've met one person with Autism, then you've only met one person with Autism." While this is completely accurate, there seems to be common attribute, the need to recharge. They need to recharge so they can love the world with their entire soul and being. When your child is acting 'weird' or 'not themselves,' it's not that at all. They are preparing their heart, mind, and soul to love you where you are in life and the world around them. Give them that space! Second, I hope you see that YOU as the parent need to consistently be part of their world. I know this is easier said than done, but is it that difficult? Our 'Ausome' loved ones have built another world that only exists for those who know that they are not perfect, who strive to see the good in people every day, and for those who look forward to a bright tomorrow, even in the bleak surroundings of today. Sounds familiar, right? We as neurotypical people strive to reach these goals and mindsets every day. We turn to self-help, motivational speakers, etc. However, for some of us, we have been blessed with a tangible key to our purpose: to not be in this world, but be in their world.

Find out more about Jamiel Owens here:

Facebook: The Ausome Show and Ausomeness Inc.
Instagram: @theausomeshow and @ausomenessinc
Linkedin: https://www.linkedin.com/in/
jamiel-owens-75a985213/

STORY 22:
Nicole Pasker

Mom, Advocate
Favorite Superhero: My daughter Shyanne (Cayden's big sister)

"I can't do this anymore." That is exactly what I was thinking as I slid down the wall where I crumbled into one big heaping pile of 'Hot Mess Mama.' As a child, I just figured that motherhood would be my career when I grew up. Being a Mom was all I wanted to be. I saw myself loving and nurturing kids and helping them grow into who they were supposed to be in life. In my pile of 'Hot Mess Mama,' I was wondering if I could even do this anymore. I felt like I was failing at the one thing I had dreamed of being since I was a child.

At this time in my life, I had three kids and was freshly divorced after a ten-year marriage. My eldest daughter, Shyanne, was 6 years old. My youngest son, Levi, was 1 and my son, Cayden, was 3 years old at the time. Cayden didn't talk and I was unable to control him (Cayden refers to those years as his Tazmanian Devil years). Cayden was later diagnosed with ADHD, ODD (Oppositional defiant disorder), and low-functioning autism. On the night when I questioned everything about myself (the pile of 'Hot Mess Mama' night), I had a rough day with my son, and I just didn't have any answers anymore.

We had just recently moved into a brand-new apartment after being homeless for about 2 months. (that's a whole other story). I had recently met an amazing woman, April. She had twins diagnosed with autism and they seemed to be doing really well. April shared with me that her twins were previously non-verbal and also struggled with explosive meltdowns.

April did so well, not only with the twins, but all five of her kids. She would share with me all that she was doing so I could help my son every time I came over. On that night, I remember calling April and just sobbing for a long time before I could speak. When I did, I asked April if she would please consider adopting my son because as much as I wanted to help my son, I believed the only way to help him was to give him to someone who had the resources and knowledge to help him.

April came to my home that night, and we engaged in a lengthy and heartfelt conversation. Throughout our discussion, she lovingly cared for Cayden, providing a sense of comfort and reassurance. When it was time for her to leave, she looked me in the eyes and offered the following words, "I understand that you may feel like you've fallen short as a mother. However, I also see you as an incredibly strong, wonderful, and amazing mom who is willing to do whatever it takes to secure the proper help for her child, even if that means someone else raises him. Before we make any permanent decisions, would you be willing to let my husband and I mentor you and your son over the next few months? Let's see where this journey takes us. If, in the end, you still wish to proceed with adoption, it would be my privilege to raise him." Overwhelmed with gratitude, I replied, "Yes, I will do that. Thank you so much."

Over the course of several months, April worked closely with both of us, providing guidance and support both collectively and individually. She patiently taught me how to tune into Cayden's communication, deciphering his intentions through his behaviors. April emphasized the significance of nutrition in Cayden's progress and encouraged the transition to natural, wholesome options whenever feasible.

Cayden's sister, Shyanne, has also played a pivotal role in aiding him. Shyanne possesses a remarkable ability to connect with Cayden in ways that I am still learning. Their sibling bond is truly remarkable, and I eagerly anticipate the day when they can share their extraordinary journey as brother and sister with the world.

Cayden and I would like to convey an important message to the world, being autistic does not equate to being broken, and it certainly does not imply a lack of understanding about what is said or happening around them. In Cayden's own words, "Just because I may not know how to verbalize something does not mean I do not understand. I just may not understand it in the same way you expect me to."

Reflecting on our journey, there are numerous aspects I wish I had access to when Cayden was younger, particularly in terms of support and securing the necessary funding for his well-being and development. Much of the progress we've made for Cayden has been a collective effort involving myself, his devoted big sister, Shyanne, and the compassionate individuals we've encountered along the way—individuals who have become cherished members of our extended family, lovingly referred to as 'Aunts' and 'Uncles.'

I hope the world recognizes the immense importance of a community in nurturing and supporting an autistic child, and how thriving becomes possible when that support network is in place. Our journey has been marked by various elements that have significantly contributed to Cayden's speech development and behavioral progress. Above all, this journey has been guided by boundless patience, love, and an abundance of grace in all its colors.

One remarkable aspect of our journey has been dietary adjustments, and a program that made a remarkable difference in Cayden's speech development is known as "Baby Can Read." I wholeheartedly recommend it for every child, as it has played a pivotal role in Cayden's growth.

Cayden's superhero is undoubtedly his sister, Shyanne, and I wholeheartedly concur. One day, I aspire to repay her for everything she has done for both me and my son, her beloved brother, Cayden. I must also acknowledge Cayden's younger brother, who has played a significant role in Cayden's upbringing. His extraordinary patience and unwavering support have been instrumental in our journey.

On that pivotal day when April offered to mentor my son and me, all I truly yearned for was the reassurance that I could do this, that I was capable of raising him. April provided the sanctuary I needed, both for myself and my son. She asked for nothing in return, and she, along with her family, enveloped us in their love and support, treating my son, my other children, and me like cherished family members.

I understand that there will be challenging days, and perhaps even prolonged seasons, when Cayden and I face uncertain waters together. However, I now possess an unwavering confidence that reverberates within me, proclaiming, "I GOT THIS," no matter what lies ahead. My earnest hope is that if you ever find yourself in need of such support, you will reach out and engage in an honest conversation with someone who can help guide you on your journey. If you yearn to rediscover that sense of empowerment and exude the "I GOT THIS" vibe for yourself and your family, let's talk. My specialty is standing in the gap with, and for, families. I can guide you through the process of raising what I fondly refer to as "special superhero children." Just as April once walked alongside me, I'm passionate about offering support to families.

Find out more about Nicole Pasker here:

B2hopecoaching@gmail.com

STORY 23:
Donna Richards

Mom, Advocate
Favorite Superhero: Chef Justin

When Justin was young, professionals delivered a prognosis that left our family devastated. They told us that Justin was, "severe and profoundly mentally retarded" and that, "he will never have speech and will more than likely be in an institution by age 18." It was a grim and disheartening prediction. However, life often has a way of defying expectations and proving experts wrong.

Hello, I'm Donna Richards, and Chef Justin is our youngest son, the caboose of our family. Our journey has been one of challenges, resilience, and ultimately, triumph. We are a close-knit family with two sons serving in the Army, one in the Marine Corps, and one who became an angel when we tragically lost him at the age of 17 in 2013.

Justin's early years were marked by significant struggles. He had daily meltdowns and severe allergies, which added to the complexity of his condition. Born just 13 months after his brother Jace, who was later diagnosed with Asperger's, Justin initially appeared to be a happy child. However, everything changed after he received his two-year-old MMR (measles, mumps, and rubella) vaccination. Justin had a severe reaction to the vaccine, which manifested as a high fever and chills, and he was never the same again.

Following this traumatic event, Justin lost his ability to speak and had to rely on sign language to communicate. He attended daycare and later joined a specialized program designed for children with autism. In an effort to provide him with additional support, we purchased a horse farm in Alabama, where he could engage in equine therapy, which has been known to be beneficial for individuals on the autism spectrum.

Over the years, we dedicated ourselves to helping Justin through Applied Behavior Analysis (ABA) therapy and numerous other interventions. At age five, his brother Jace wrote a heartwarming book titled "My Brother's Keeper: A Kindergartner's View of Autism," which garnered significant attention and even reached the number one spot in 2005. It was an early testament to the love and support that surrounded Justin within our family.

Justin's journey took an unexpected turn when he was 16. He expressed a keen interest in cooking and requested a subscription box from Blue Apron, a meal kit delivery service. At the time, most of us had never heard of this concept. Justin began cooking three meals a week using Blue Apron and later added HelloFresh to his culinary repertoire. Eventually, we switched to Epicure, a gluten-free meal kit subscription.

Cooking became Justin's passion. He was drawn to its precision and rule-oriented nature, where exact measurements and adherence to recipes were essential. Despite still having moments influenced by his autism, Justin was determined to turn his passion for cooking into a career.

The pivotal moment arrived when Justin decided he wanted to attend culinary school. The prospect was exciting yet nerve-wracking for our family. Could he handle the demands of a professional culinary program, including strict deadlines, in-depth reports, and rigorous testing? As it turned out, Justin not only handled it but excelled in all areas.

As Justin pursued his culinary dreams, he encountered numerous challenges and hurdles along the way. The demanding culinary school curriculum required not only technical skill but also effective time management and organization—areas that had historically posed challenges for Justin due to his autism.

However, what became evident as Justin pursued his culinary education was his incredible dedication and meticulous attention to detail, characteristics that are often associated with individuals on the autism spectrum. The structured and rule-oriented nature of the culinary world seemed to resonate with him, providing a clear framework within which he could excel.

He embraced the rigorous training, practiced tirelessly, and quickly gained a reputation among his instructors and peers for his unwavering commitment to perfection. Justin's innate ability to replicate complex recipes with precision was nothing short of astounding, and it became clear that his passion for cooking was not just a fleeting interest but a lifelong calling.

The culinary school experience also played a vital role in Justin's personal development. It helped him build social skills and confidence in interacting with colleagues and mentors, something he had struggled with earlier in life due to his autism. The collaborative nature of a professional kitchen environment exposed him to diverse personalities and taught him the importance of effective communication and teamwork.

Despite the success and recognition he achieved during his culinary journey, Justin has remained humble and grounded. He understands that his journey is not only about personal achievement but also about inspiring others. Through his social media platforms, "Autism Family Circus," he has become a source of inspiration and support for individuals and families affected by autism. He shares not only his culinary creations but also his personal experiences, offering a glimpse into the daily triumphs and challenges of life on the autism spectrum.

In addition to his culinary pursuits, Justin's story underscores the importance of continued research and understanding of autism spectrum disorders. While his journey has been remarkable, it also serves as a reminder that early intervention and access to appropriate therapies can make a significant difference in the lives of individuals with autism.

As a family, we are committed to raising awareness about autism and providing resources to support other families on similar journeys. Our blog, autismfamilycircus.com, serves as a platform for sharing insights, tips, and information on autism-related topics. We firmly believe that by sharing our experiences and knowledge, we can contribute to a more inclusive and understanding world.

In conclusion, Chef Justin's journey from an early diagnosis of severe autism to becoming a successful culinary professional is a testament to the power of determination, love, and the unwavering support of a family who refused to accept the limitations that experts once predicted. His story serves as an inspiration to individuals with autism and their families, reminding them that with the right opportunities, dedication, and a supportive network, anything is possible. Justin's passion for cooking has not only transformed his life but has also touched the lives of many, proving that autism does not define a person but rather adds a unique and valuable perspective to the world.

Find out more about Donna Richards here:

https://autismfamilycircus.com/

STORY 24:
Maria Alejandra Rincón

Autistic Adult, Advocate
Favorite Superhero: Spider Man

My favorite superhero is Spider-Man. I feel like I can relate to Spider-Man so much. Like Spider-Man/Peter Parker, I can be a brilliant student/worker but lazy and irresponsible at times. Also, like Spider-Man, I was, and still am, a nerdy girl. I always thought it was cool how Spider-Man was the first teenage superhero when normally teenagers were sidekicks in comics. He never had a mentor like other superheroes which was also cool.

I was diagnosed with autism at the age of three. I was told by therapists and some preschool teachers that I was never going to be a normal person nor that I would ever be able to function normally in society and never be worth more than a cashier behind a register. Many people said these things and more to my parents throughout my life. At the time, I was too young to understand why I had to be in a special education class or why I had to be in therapy. I had a unique way of seeing the world in a way that was difficult to explain. It was not until later in life that I started to notice and wonder as to why I was treated a little differently than the other kids. I remember having autistic meltdowns as a child or suffering from sensory overload. I have always throughout my whole life been socially awkward and seen as an outsider. It has always been hard to relate to other people due to me seeing things differently or having interests that may seem 'odd' or 'outdated.' For example, a lot of my peers like modern music or shows like "The Bachelorette." I cannot stand a lot of today's music and I do not like a lot of the shows everyone else watches. I have special interests such as Disney, Star Wars, Marvel comics, dogs, and music from the 60s, 70s, and 80s.

Another challenge of mine is understanding emotions, knowing how to react in social situations, or understanding sarcasm. I will admit that even as an adult, I do struggle with those things at times. I would be lying to you if I said there have not been times when I must Google how to react or what to say in a certain social situation. There are also moments that I still have where I just sit there wondering if I had taken the appropriate reaction to the situation or if I had said the right thing. It can become an issue to the point where I overthink things a lot. Even as an adult, I still find myself being overly stimulated at times and suffering from sensory overload. I also struggle with social anxiety a lot and while I have learned to socialize over the years, it can be hard at times for me to approach people. One of the areas that I am slowly improving is communication. For many years, communication was one thing I constantly struggled with, especially expressing how I felt. Growing up with autism made me feel like I was a burden on everyone else's lives.

For the longest time, I hated myself and thought I had no purpose in this world. I had sadly become used to people saying mean things to my face and behind my back. I even had some students say things to me like, "You do realize you're autistic, right?" I would also hear comments like, "I'm sorry, we don't like special needs people." One year, I had a student even snatch my yearbook from my hands and wrote, "Don't kill yourself." I remember how later in high school, I had to eat lunch alone in the bathroom while everyone else would eat in the cafeteria. However, that was nothing compared to the deep depression I experienced in my early adult years. I felt like I didn't deserve to live, and everyone would be better off without me, and I had so much trauma that I even became suicidal. Luckily, I failed in that.

It took me many years to finally be open about having autism and coming to accept it. It was something I always tried to hide. I was masking for most of my life and always felt ashamed or uncomfortable if anyone ever brought up the subject. However, in 2018, I finally came out to the public as an autistic person in an Instagram post. It had to be one of the bravest things I had ever done in my whole life. After I had come out to the public about my autism, I felt a huge sigh of relief.

I wish the world knew how autism is truly a God-given gift. While this may be a topic of debate by many people in the autism community, I consider autism my superpower. I'm not implying that I don't experience challenging days (believe me, I do), or that all autistic individuals are savants. However, I refer to autism as my superpower because it grants me a unique perspective and enables me to recognize the beauty in aspects of life that often go unnoticed by others. I appreciate the smallest of things that people think little about. For example, there can be a person who is not considered 'conventionally attractive' by society while I can see that face as beautiful and deeply appreciate it. I will think to myself, "Wow, that is a really nice face." Another example is when my fiancé asks where I would like to eat, and I choose a simple casual restaurant such as Chipotle. My fiancé will question it because he had intended to take me to a nicer restaurant, but I will be the happiest and most excited going to Chipotle. I hope the world could recognize the simplicity and gratitude that many individuals on the autism spectrum possess.

One unfair assumption that people make about autistic people is how we allegedly lack empathy and only care about ourselves. The idea of that is absurd to me. Of course, we care. We just show our empathy in our own way. It may be hard for us to express how we feel at that moment, or we do not take immediate action at the moment. If anything, I think people on the spectrum like me are the most empathetic. There are times when we can be overly empathetic. We often sense another person's emotions more intensely. We have what is known as 'affective empathy'. Affective empathy is based on instincts and involuntary responses to the emotions of others. It can be overwhelming and strong. One perfect example is how we act overly empathetic towards animals or smaller children. Especially towards animals, autistic people are known to have a deep connection with animals.

The most important point I wish the world understood about autism is the non-judgmental nature of individuals on the spectrum. We rarely care for social expectations due to our perception of the world. We are so busy being passionate about other things or we perceive the world in such a literal way that we will never judge you based on how you look, your past, what you are wearing, or your financial situation. Many people have confided in me because they felt like they could tell me anything and I would not judge them. I would listen to them intently. We know what it is like to be judged on looks or material things. We are often excluded from our peers due to not conforming to social norms or being made fun of for our special interests. When will people understand that we don't want to spread that negativity in our environment? We accept your differences, but we ask that you accept us for our differences.

I hope to one day be on a talk show such as "Good Morning America." I would love to one day write a book about my experiences with autism and discuss it on a talk show. I want to improve my public speaking and combat my shyness so I can share my story with the world. I want to not only help people on the autism spectrum, but I also dream of helping people with mental health issues. I want to be that person that they can confide in. I want to be a safe space for anyone who is struggling mentally; especially with the people who are feeling suicidal. It breaks my heart how many people in this world end their lives by suicide every day. I dream of one day also starting a suicide prevention support group. I'd also like to initiate a support group for individuals dealing with autism, mental health challenges, thoughts of suicide, or simply anyone experiencing anxiety and seeking companionship. It would be a positive, like-minded environment where everyone is welcome. It would teach people with autism how to socialize. It would be a safe space for people with autism or anxiety to feel comfortable. I have always hated the idea of cliques in high school so, this would also be a way of going against cliques and just having an environment where everyone can feel accepted. No matter who you are, you will always be welcome to my support group.

Find out more about Maria Alejandra Rincón here:

Instagram: @mariaarincon_tcb

STORY 25:
Vincent Rinicella

Autistic Adult, Advocate, and Speaker
Favorite Superhero: The Hulk

My name is Vince Rinicella and I am a 23-year-old adult with a form of autism that does not allow me to communicate verbally. This is called non-speaking autism or being a non-speaker. This has affected me my entire life, presenting me with both challenges and success-es. Navigating a life with autism is not for the faint of heart. Like our favorite superheroes, you must be hardworking, resilient, and determined to beat the odds and prove the naysayers wrong. These qualities are why many people draw comparisons between superhe-roes and autistics. We too, are often underestimated or overlooked until given the chance to prove our worth. I truly believe there lies a superhero within every single person affected by autism, and our stories are equally inspiring and deserve to be shared.

You may wonder how my apraxic body works. When I was a little boy, my body was a dysregulated mess. My brain had very little con-trol over it, and my body ran on impulse. I could not keep my body still or focused no matter how much I tried. My mouth would often hum, and my hands would clap together as a way to calm the chaos inside of me. I frequently eloped to the extent that my parents joked about installing an invisible fence. I think there is a misconception about some of the causes of why young children with autism engage in unsafe behavior. Many professionals would say that we are unaware of what is unsafe. Personally, this was not the case for me, I knew when I was swinging too recklessly or climbing on things I shouldn't. What I didn't know was how to stop my body from craving the sensory input that came with those unsafe behaviors. This is where occupational therapy was instrumental in helping me. I was able to find ways to get the input my body needed to soothe without being unsafe. This, along with a clean diet did wonders to regulate my unruly body.

The toughest challenge that I have experienced is not having the ability to speak verbally due to a motor disorder common to those with autism. The natural way of communicating is through your mouth by producing speech. My motor system just does not work like that because of breakdowns between my brain and my body. Beginning with sign language, to picture exchange cards, then Augmentative and Alternative Communication (AAC) devices, my teachers, therapists, and family tried many different methods to help me successfully communicate. AAC helped me to request items, but I still could not express my thoughts or have a conversation, which is what I longed for the most. Fortunately, my communication was fully unlocked once I learned how to spell on the letterboard and type on the keyboard. I now have conversations daily with loved ones, I speak at conferences to advocate for non-speakers, and I have made meaningful connections with friends who are non-speaking and neurotypical. I never thought my life would turn out this way, and I feel so grateful for the trained professionals who taught me the skills needed to connect my brain and body.

The biggest misconception surrounding autism is that it is an intellectual disability. This is far from the truth. Not only is our cognition perfectly intact, but many individuals on the autism spectrum are also highly intelligent. The struggle comes from not having any means to display our intelligence because of a condition called apraxia. This is a fancy way of saying our bodies cannot execute the directions our brains are sending to us. Apraxia impacts every aspect of our lives but mostly limits our communication. This causes an inaccurate display of our intellect, which directly impacts how we appear to others. The next time you meet or see somebody with autism who appears as though they can't communicate, you need to assume the direct opposite. Interact with them the same way you would a neurotypical person that is the same age. We are in here and deserve to be treated as such.

We all have legitimate goals we want to accomplish in life. My goal in life is to advocate for non-speakers. I began working towards my high school diploma just over a year ago, to be exposed to the vast amount of information I missed out on in my school setting due to being a non-speaker. My dream is to stop this from happening to others. I plan to go to college to pursue a degree in political science.

The first stop for me will be to go to community college to get used to college life. I want to finish with a degree from a university. With my degree, I plan to go to my state capitol and fight for the rights of non-speakers like me. This change needs to occur at the state level with our public school system. Communication is a basic human right and needs to be fought for regarding those with apraxia. My ultimate goal is to be a superhero for non-speakers by fighting for this at the federal level.

If I had to pick a favorite superhero, I would choose the Hulk. I identify and sympathize with his origin story. Bruce Banner is a quiet, but intelligent man. He was empathetic to the extent of risking his life to save somebody else. It is convenient for people to forget that the Hulk didn't turn green, grow ten times his size, and start hulk smashing everything just for the fun of it. It is something that his body does that is beyond his control. He is reacting to poison. We all become the worst versions of ourselves after a poisonous experience. Living with non-speaking autism may have made me taste poison at times, but it did not stop me from becoming my own superhero.

Find out more about Vincent Rinicella here:

https://theunfilteredmindofvincent.wordpress.com/

STORY 26:
Jeremy, Johnathan and Corrine Rochford

Autistic Dad, Speaker, Coach, Advocate
Favorite Superhero: My children, Johnathan and Corinne

I'll never forget when I was first introduced to "autism." I was picking up my son from preschool, and the director called me over to let me know she had some concerns. Concerns that she thought my son might be a little 'different' than the rest of the students. Little did I know that within just a few months, not only would my son be diagnosed with ASD, but my daughter would be as well. And months after that, so would I. Within a span of two years, we went from a family of four who knew next to nothing about 'life on the spectrum' to a family of four where 75% of us are Autistic. We're so 'on the spectrum' now that my son must remind his mother how sorry he is every April that everyone else will be celebrated (during Autism Awareness Month) except for her.

But that we still love her anyway. :)

To say my children have changed my life would be an understatement. Seeing the world through their Autistic eyes allowed me to see life through my own. It forced me to become a better husband, father, and overall human. Because of that, I am forever grateful. For those reasons and many others, my children, Johnathan and Corinne, are my favorite superheroes.

Not only because of their impact on my life but because they dare to be themselves. My daughter, for example, when asked if she would like to contribute to this chapter, literally jumped at the chance. Here's what she had to say about some of the challenges of growing up on the spectrum and what she'd like the world to know.

> *"There are a lot of challenges with having autism. Sometimes, when doing a math equation for school, I can mess up the problem, misinterpret the question, and answer it incorrectly. Kids at school can make fun of me because of my Autism. I'm more sensitive, so this makes me an easier target for being picked on. I wish the world would understand that we think differently and won't think of things as they do. Most neurotypical people believe that autism is a disorder. Technically, they are right, but I think otherwise. In my eyes, autism is a superpower. I dream to be a professional entertainer on the Disney cruise ships. My favorite superhero is Supergirl."*
>
> *-Corinne Rochford (Age 11 & Autistic)*

And then there is my son, who hopes to work for LEGO as a 'Master Builder.' He wasn't afraid to share his thoughts about growing up on the spectrum as well.

"I wish people would understand that they don't have to say, "I'm sorry you have autism." I mean, why would you say that? Don't they know that being Autistic makes you super cool? Like, there are a lot of famous people who are autistic, and when I grow up, I'm going to be one of them. I even heard them say that Albert Einstein was probably autistic. I just wish people knew that being autistic is Legendary, Epic, and Awesome."

"There are some challenges, though. Sometimes, I'll feel stressed over normal things. Like when I have to go to therapy while other kids are playing on the playground or learning something cool in Mr. Bostic's class. I do feel like I'm missing out during those times. It's also hard sometimes when I get dysregulated. But then I remember how loved I feel with my family and friends and that makes everything OK."

"When thinking about my favorite superhero, I have to say, I pick them all. Why? Because superheroes are like cookies. Each one offers something different and special. Not better, not worse. So they're all awesome. And, because of that, how can you have a favorite?"

-Johnathan Rochford (Age 8 & Autistic)

Seeing the world through their eyes brings me to what I wish the world knew about autism, which is that being autistic doesn't mean you're deficient; it simply means that your brain sees the world differently than others.

I look at it like a Mac vs. a PC.

One isn't better than the other; they're just different. But different in the best way possible. And because of their differences, they can complement each other and push the world forward. Now, that doesn't mean you won't have to take a few extra steps to get Microsoft Office to run smoothly on a MAC. But it's very possible. That's what makes me so excited about the time we're living in right now. We know more than we've ever known about autism and will continue to learn more. As a society, we've got such a bright and amazing future.

But I don't just feel that way about my kids.

I feel that way about you.

And your kids.

Collectively, we're part of a generation who can change this world for the better if we, as adults and parents, do our best to harness the brilliance of our autistic selves and our autistic youth. Yes, some challenges come with being on the spectrum. Still, they do not outweigh the intelligence, capability, and sheer resiliency that these individuals have. So, if you're autistic or are the parent or loved one of someone who is, take heart and understand you're genuinely a part of something special. Yes, we autistics have some quirks and do some things that the rest of the world might consider 'odd.' But let's be honest, there are many things that 'neurotypicals' do that I find a little silly as well.

But that's OK because that's 'normal' to them.

And we're 'normal' to us.

And that's OK because this world needs both Macs and PCs to thrive.

So, no matter where you are on the spectrum, please know that you are seen, loved, & appreciated just the way you are. In the eyes of me and my family, we think you're Legendary, Epic, and Awesome.

Find out more about Jeremy Rochford here:

www.OurNeuroFam.com

STORY 27:
Heidi Rome

Mom, Advocate, Author
Favorite Superhero: Wonder Woman

My son Ethan, 18, is severely affected by autism. His limited verbal skills, sensitivity to loud sounds, and sudden changes, along with his dysregulated episodes, have been challenging since infancy. Unlike portrayals of milder forms of autism in the media, Ethan's experiences are rarely shown or understood by the masses.

When Ethan received his diagnosis, it propelled me into a frenzied race to find solutions, with society's 'good mother' narrative pressing heavily on me, tying my worth to his 'cure.' This urgency was deepened by a devastating assessment from a leading autism center, claiming five-year-old Ethan had the mental capacity of a five-month-old baby. This verdict not only shattered me but reshaped our relationship, reinforcing my belief that my primary duty was to fix and change Ethan. Isn't that what Wonder Woman would have done if the writers had seen fit to work an autistic child into her movie script?

Doctors and therapists of every variety surrounded us, recommending extensive therapies. As Ethan transitioned from early intervention into the school system, we found ourselves battling for a suitable educational environment for him and noticed our support network dwindling. Friends and family distanced themselves, put off by the unfamiliar challenges we faced, even as new, unexpected supporters (Angels! Super Friends!) emerged.

The public's perception of autism has also shifted over time. Many now view autism as a quirky trait, often glorified by media portrayals. In my view, the broadening definition of the autism spectrum has diluted its meaning, making it less actionable and reducing the urgency to provide support. This evolving view of autism, while seeming inclusive, has detrimental implications. When society perceives autism as merely a 'difference' rather than a 'disability,' it undermines the very real challenges faced by those with severe autism. This perspective threatens the tangible support and resources these individuals desperately need.

Ethan's reality, and that of many others, is stark. He requires constant care and struggles with basic daily activities. While he is indeed a unique and wonderful individual, the challenges he faces cannot be downplayed. As we advocate for inclusivity and understanding, it's crucial to remember that the needs of the severely autistic community must not be overlooked.

Upon Ethan's diagnosis of autism, a term that encompasses a vast range of experiences, our lives took an immediate turn. It's vital to understand that the necessities of a severely autistic child are different from a high-functioning autistic adult. Every individual deserves respect and love, but to genuinely support them, we must address their unique needs holistically – emotionally, financially, and physically.

Autism isn't transient; it's lifelong. We cannot let the commendable ethos of equality blur the distinct needs of those severely affected by autism. Terms like 'disabled,' 'vulnerable,' and 'apraxia' aren't derogatory; they spotlight the real challenges some face, underscoring the gap between their current situation and where society needs to be.

When Ethan's autism diagnosis reverberated in my ears, it felt like my life's joy was stolen, replaced by an era of trepidation. I threw myself into the role of the 'Good Mother,' scouring every available therapy and approach, hoping to find a way to liberate Ethan and me from this consuming cycle of hope and despair. Isn't that the role of a superhero, to be the savior who swoops in and saves the day in the nick of time?

Ethan's first school, a proponent of Applied Behavioral Analysis (ABA), promised transformation. We believed this to be the answer, suppressing any apprehensions we had about Ethan's personalized needs. But as time went on, his aggressive behaviors persisted, and the school blamed our 'leniency,' pushing us further into stricter regimens.

Our relationship with Ethan mutated. No longer just his mother, I became an enforcer, partnering with the school to change Ethan. It felt like I was betraying his trust, and my own identity as a parent became fractured. I grappled with guilt, yet I was too terrified to change our course. The school's tactics, shrouded in secrecy and unyielding discipline, seemed like our only hope. At any price.

Outside of school, I embarked on a frenzy of treatments and consultations, desperate to find a cure. From stem cell transplants to dolphin therapy, no avenue was left unexplored. The pressure was suffocating. Expert opinions and polished marketing tactics clouded my judgment. Desperation and fear clouded my every thought, painting a grim future for Ethan. I had dreams of myself bleeding out on the street, detached strangers passing by. Gasping, no solace anywhere, I sought light in my despair. It was survival; it was life or death, and I felt that God was busy with other things.

Despite our relentless endeavors, Ethan wasn't improving. The mounting appointments and treatments were draining, emotionally and financially. I felt isolated, my anguish unnoticed by the world. As Ethan grew older, his school's ABA methods intensified, focusing heavily on physical restraint. I felt ensnared between society's ideal of the 'Good Mother' and the pull of my own maternal instincts. Would the real Wonder Woman please step forward? Ahhh–she did. I did. With each passing night, the inner voice demanding change grew stronger. The spell of entrusting Ethan entirely to the school's doctrine finally cracked.

With newfound clarity, we enrolled Ethan in a school with a di-ametrically opposite approach. Here, behaviors were viewed as communication from kids lacking spoken language. The focus was on deciphering their needs and offering them alternative ways to communicate. The school's motto, "Presume competence," radiated an optimism we had longed for.

This transition seemed like a step forward, yet the changing paradigm brought me to question the message I realized I had been sending him for years: He was broken, he was abnormal, his very existence pained me, and Mom thought she had to sacrifice everything, even her happiness, to change him. Ouch!

Ethan's shift to a new school, which emphasized relationship-building and play over strict behavior modification, was a breath of fresh air. It was my opportunity to reclaim my 'Wonder Woman' identity, prioritizing Ethan's wellbeing over societal judgments. While therapy still consumed us, the transparency and hope of this new direction was a powerful relief. The school introduced assistive communication techniques, revealing for the first time Ethan's high intelligence. He spelled out feelings and thoughts, such as, "Basking in joy," and had conversations that deeply refuted and contrasted with the prior 'expert' determination of his limited cognition.

However, even though Ethan could communicate with devices, his dysregulated, injurious behaviors continued to escalate as he entered puberty at age 11. The walls of the house were shattered from Ethan's head-banging, and we were bruised from being hit or kicked during outbursts. We made the heart-wrenching decision for our beloved child to move to an out-of-state, residential therapeutic school where he could have the 24/7 trained and caring support he needed and that we, his exhausted family, could not provide to keep him and us safe. Despite my sadness and sense of loss before his departure, Ethan shared that he felt brave. He shared, "Don't be sad for me" and asked, "Are quitters a failure or choosing a different path to success?" A profound conversation with the aid of Ethan's assistive communication device then followed:

Ethan: "God is in my heart and He will always protect me."

Me: "Did He tell you that?"

Ethan: "When I lived in heaven, He told me that."

Me: "Do you remember that time?"

Ethan: "When I lived with God, I wasn't named Ethan yet."

Me: "What was your name?"

Ethan: "I was not to remember it. I had many before."

Me: "Do you recall anything from that time?"

Ethan: "I remember life with no body. In heaven, there are no bodies. Just spectacular energy."

Me: "Did you choose to come here as Ethan Rome?"

Ethan: "Yes. I picked to be me and have many challenges."

Me: "Did you pick us as your family?"

Ethan: "We were family another time. We didn't live here. We lived in a small group but got hurt by warriors."

Me: "Why did you choose to come back with challenges?"

Ethan: "I will be greatly rewarded in eternity."

Me: "How can we help you?"

Ethan: "I have to complete my journey as prescribed by God."

Me: "Does it feel longer than you thought it would be?"

Ethan: "Yes. The journey is unfathomably longer than expected."

Me: "What can we do to help you?"

Ethan: "You just have to love me and that is your job. The rest is my job to do."

His words resonated deeply, bringing tears to my eyes. "You just have to love me," he said. All these years, I had been trying to change Ethan instead of accepting him. Ethan, once labeled as having the cognition of an infant, was revealing profound spiritual insights. This conversation transformed and uplifted me. I no longer saw Ethan as a project to fix. He was a complete human, rich in wisdom and awareness. Ethan's challenges and strengths coexisted, making him who he is: a unique human, crafted in God's image. This realization allowed me to shed the weight of the distorted 'Good Mother' persona. Today, Ethan is blossoming in a nurturing environment. He has grown calmer and the dysregulated behaviors, their messages received, have abated and receded. Witnessing Ethan's unfolding has affirmed our choices, reminding us that, when guided by love and understanding rather than a 'fix,' we illuminate the right path forward.

When love is our North Star, both Mom and her autistic child of any age can each step into their true superhero identities, accepting and loving each other for all of who they are, as spiritual beings each having their own human experience.

Find out more about Heidi Rome here:

You Just Have to Love Me: Mothering Instructions From My Autistic Child
https://www.momsspectrumoasis.com/
LinkedIn: https://www.linkedin.com/in/
heidi-rome-8b60a110/

STORY 28:
Richard and Karoline Schreiber

Dad, Advocate

Favorite Superhero: My daughter Karoline

Parenthood is a remarkable journey, filled with love, challenges, learning, and ceaseless advocacy, especially when parenting a child on the autism spectrum. My name is Richard Schreiber, and I am a father and a devoted autism advocate. This journey has led me to a profound understanding of the complexities and needs of individuals on the autism spectrum, particularly through the experiences of my daughter, Karoline.

The Autism Innovation Community Network, which I founded, is driven by a core mantra: "to provide holistic, innovative, and technology-driven autism support." This approach stands in contrast to the mainstream autism services that most families are directed toward such as pharmaceutical options and standardized behavioral analysis services.

Our journey took a poignant turn when Karoline was diagnosed with autism at the age of seven, thanks to her first-grade teacher's keen observation of autism symptoms. The post-diagnosis period was a rollercoaster of emotions, from confusion and uncertainty to an unwavering determination to find the best possible support for Karoline. We delved into the available autism services, hoping to find the sanctuary of support and guidance we needed, but our initial experiences were disheartening.

The diagnosis phase was marked by a whirlwind of emotions and immediate adjustments. It was a period of struggle, revelation, and realization that, as parents, we were our daughter's true advocates, regardless of her challenges and special needs. We understood that if our child had special needs, she needed our support, love, and advocacy more than ever.

However, the path forward was far from straightforward. Initially, we were led down a well-intentioned but misleading path, filled with misleading information, misaligned services, and a lack of genuine understanding of the multifaceted nature of autism. We encountered services that embraced a one-size-fits-all approach, inadvertently sidelining the unique needs, strengths, and potential of children like Karoline.

At the recommendation of pediatricians and school advisors, we pursued pharmaceutical intervention and enrolled Karoline in Applied Behavioral Analysis (ABA) services. These services often followed a cookie-cutter approach, and we occasionally had to intervene with counselors to ensure our daughter was not pushed to suppress her unique behaviors.

The outcome of these interventions was far from what we had hoped for. The drugs and ABA services left Karoline feeling like a shell of herself, devoid of the individuality and dignity we cherished. It was a painful realization that left a lasting impact on our family. As a parent, witnessing your child in such a state is a burden that remains etched in memory.

This experience served as a wake-up call for our family. We knew we had to take matters into our own hands, navigating through the overwhelming sea of information and resources to find a path tailored to Karoline's unique needs. This marked the beginning of a more informed, personalized, and nuanced approach to autism support and therapy—one that celebrated Karoline's individuality while addressing her challenges.

Karoline's mother, Maggie Schreiber, became an expert in essential oils and discovered a combination that proved transformative for Karoline, reducing her symptoms and restoring her sense of self. Additionally, enrolling Karoline in the Brain Balance program, which incorporated nutrition, diet, exercise, music, and other non-intrusive activities, contributed significantly to her development. These interventions helped improve her hand-eye coordination and other attributes, enabling her to flourish.

Empowered by our knowledge and lived experiences, our family transitioned into fervent autism advocates. We channeled our insights and learning into building a community that prioritized understanding, acceptance, and tailored support. We founded the New York City Autism Community—a group where families navigating the autism journey could find unwavering support, validated information, and a network that genuinely comprehended the diverse aspects and spectrums of autism. This community, with over 1200 members in a closed Facebook Group, has become a source of strength and assistance for many.

Before the COVID-19 pandemic, our group organized meetings where families and autistic children and young adults could come together to play, engage in activities, stroll through Central Park, and simply be themselves. It was a space where parents could connect, share experiences, and offer one another much-needed support.

Our journey, though challenging, serves as a testament to the resilience of parents, the boundless potential of children on the spectrum, and the profound impact of a supportive, knowledgeable community. Our family's story is a beacon of hope, resilience, and a steadfast call for continued advocacy and systemic change in the realm of autism services.

To provide further insight into our journey, we sat down with Karoline to get her perspective:

When were you diagnosed?

Karoline: My memory's kind of fuzzy, but I think I was diagnosed in kindergarten. My parents and teacher were talking about it, and they got me diagnosed when I was a bit older.

What challenges have you faced?

Karoline: Spelling is a big challenge for me. I'm good at other school stuff, like math and art (I love drawing cartoons!). My memory isn't great either. I forget things quickly if I don't do them right away. My mom spoke Spanish to me all my life, and I never really picked it up. Also, when it comes to cooking and stuff, if she shows me, it's like the information goes in one ear and out the other. I need things written down or shown to me multiple times to understand.

What should people know about those living with autism?

Karoline: Just be nice to us, okay? Everyone's different. Loud sounds don't bother me, but they might bother someone else with autism. We're not all the same. Some autistic people might not be nice, but anyone can be unkind, you know? Just see us as people, treat us as people, and please be patient. We're just like anyone else who needs help.

What are you most proud of?

Karoline: My report card is pretty cool; I'm smart. And I love creating stories and characters through my art. It's fun, and I'm really proud of it. It's super nice.

What are your future dreams?

Karoline: I want to create stories, whether in cartoons or video games. I've been writing a story, and I hope it becomes something. When you're inspired, it's like a one-way track, and your brain is just racing ahead.

What are your superpowers?

Karoline: Superpowers? I don't have those. I mean, being autistic doesn't give me special abilities or anything. I think differently, sure, but it's not a superpower. My brain is just wired differently, but that doesn't mean I have superpowers.

In conclusion, our journey has been a testament to the resilience of individuals on the autism spectrum and the unwavering dedication of their families. While challenges have been a part of our story, they have not defined us. Instead, we have leveraged our experiences to become advocates for change, building a community that embraces diversity, understanding, and support. We hope that our story inspires others on similar journeys to never give up hope, to embrace the uniqueness of every individual, and to work towards a more inclusive and compassionate world for those with autism.

Find out more about Richard Schreiber here:

https://www.linkedin.com/in/richardschreiber/
https://autisminnovationcommunityfoundation.org/
- events targeted to parents and caregivers of autistic members to provide access to more holistic, innovative and tech-oriented autism supports. Host of NYC Autism Tech, Innovation and Careers expo in New York City.

STORY 29:
Brigitte Shipman

Mom, Advocate, Author
Favorite Superhero: My son Joseph

I had always wanted to be a mom. When we came home with our first born, Joseph, all my dreams became a reality. He was healthy and happy.

On day 3 of being a mom, everything suddenly shifted to complete chaos. Joseph began nonstop crying. Anytime he was awake, he would literally cry. I felt helpless. Everything I tried just wouldn't soothe him. I heard from a friend that if you turn on a vacuum, it might help calm him. So, with a recording of a vacuum and his baby swing, he would slowly drift off to sleep. I can remember feeling the stress leave my body for a few moments. Then, I would get as much done as I could get done before the next shift. This was pretty much what the next 4 months of our lives looked like.

It became a bit easier once he adjusted to sleeping on his own. I did a lot of boot training crawls on the floor to reach his crib to check on him. I was so fearful that our 2 hour or more bedtime ritual would begin again if he saw me. The beginning of Joseph's life was challenging but also very rewarding. It is complex in that I had no words to explain how much I loved this human, while living in a ball of stress 24/7.

He amazed me. He had a 60 word vocabulary by the time he was 6 months old. He loved his elephants, puzzles, and many videos such as Winnie The Pooh and Disney. I understood that he loved these videos very much but what was confusing for me was that he used phrases from each one to communicate with me. It was very much like playing charades. Joseph also feared parts of these videos, but he would have meltdowns if I didn't play these videos. I also noticed that he was content as long as we stayed on a very rigid schedule. Then for the most part all was well.

I knew Joseph's intellect was way above average but once his sentences didn't form and it was obvious that he didn't know how to socially interact, I felt something was not right. I remember the day that changed motherhood and my life. It was the day that I received the diagnosis that Joseph was autistic.

Although my son didn't change overnight, my mother's heart was broken. The fear of the future took me hostage. This was my first life tsunami. It came out of nowhere and it left me disoriented and in deep pain. Grief took over, and I went in and out of grief until I learned how to heal my heart and accept our unique and beautiful life. I like to use the phrase, "How to be okay with not being okay" as acceptance.

As a pioneer mom who has navigated my own autism parenting journey, I pay forward what I have learned. I take my teaching skills and life transformation tools that I have accumulated over the past 30 plus years. These strategies help to live with more joy on the autism journey.

I picture myself at the beginning, feeling the fear and overwhelm that most parents feel, and I let her know she is going to be okay. I also forgive her for not knowing what she didn't know and for not taking better care of herself. It took me until I was in my 50s before I discovered that without taking care of myself that I would not be able to continue on the pathway that I was living. A complete shift had to happen within myself to begin the happier road to travel.

Here are my top 3 life changing discoveries that shifted my autism journey from fearful to joyful:

1. No matter what or how you navigate this journey, you will be okay. Remember that when you are living in your darkest moments. You can use this phrase as your mantra to begin, "I will be okay, we will be okay, all is well." You will feel calmer after you repeat it out loud. Mantras have helped me in some of my most stressful moments.

2. Do not compare your life to other lives. For example, when you are at a birthday party, the park, or any other social outing with your child and you are focused on how happy everyone else's life looks. This can lead to feelings of sadness rather than enjoying your own child. Rather than thinking about how easy other moms have it, shift your thinking. Notice when you go into comparison and take a breath. Then stop and give yourself love and kindness. This is part of grief, and it is trying to take you hostage. once you notice it and you are aware, then you can shift back to the joy that is right in front of you, your child.

3. Focus on yourself, self-love. Yes, I understand that this does not seem feasible when you are fighting for your child's

wellbeing. What I know for sure is that without giving yourself the self-compassion along this journey, you will experience more fatigue, stress, and wanting to escape somewhere, anywhere. Remember that if you don't fill up your own tank, you will not have any fuel left for others. Simple, but true and most difficult to incorporate in your daily life. Begin with a few minutes a day in a safe space to take a breath. Grow a ritual into daily loving care for You.

These tips helped me begin to find joy and although I have more to share with you, it is a great beginning to move through the overwhelm. Perhaps you will find your way to loving your new normal and pay your own self-discoveries forward to help other parents on their autism journeys. Once you realize that your life is its own unique beautiful experience to live, you can find peace.

ASD is not the horrible life sentence that they presented me with so many years ago. It is simply shifting the perspective of what we all imagine parenting to be and embrace what is. As Joseph once told me, "Go with the flow of the current, not against it." It is a gift to parent this exceptional person. My hope is that, if you are struggling on your autism parenting journey, you take a breath and know that your journey will be an awesome, thrilling ride, and you will be okay. Afterall, you are a superhero. Just remember to charge your energy storage along the way.

Find out more Brigitte Shipman here:

https://www.mothersguidethroughautism.com/
Book by Brigitte and Joseph Shipman "A Mother's Guide Through Autism, Through The Eyes of The Guided"

STORY 30:
Joe Shipman

Autistic Adult
Favorite Superhero: My guide, my mom

Growing up, I was a happy child who took for granted that the way I perceived and approached life was the norm, much like many others do. Of course, there were some unique experiences in my life, yet it took me a while to grasp why my reactions to the world differed from those of others and to fully comprehend the reasons behind it. From what I recall from my earliest memories, I knew what I liked and what I didn't. For a time, though, I didn't know why no one knew what I was referring to when I quoted the 1995 Pixar film, "Toy Story" or why I ran screaming at the sight of "Winnie the Pooh" in kindergarten. As I grew older, I learned that I developed differently than most people, and the way I came to interact with and view the world had a name, Autism. That's one of the names for it, anyway. When I was diagnosed as a toddler, my specific form of autism was referred to as PDD-NOS (Pervasive Developmental Disorder, Not Otherwise Specified). However, nowadays, most people commonly refer to it as ASD (Autism Spectrum Disorder).

I came to understand that autism was the reason I had particular interests in the content of my video tapes, books, trains, elephants, and a host of other things. I also realized this was why I couldn't always understand what people said, why some noises were too loud, why some foods and types of clothes were intolerable, and why I needed to be educated on the finer points of basic social skills. Over the years, I benefited from support, understanding, and acceptance. I still have struggles, but the way autism allows me to see the world, the tools I've been given, and the family I have are why I can live a healthy, purposeful, and peaceful life.

While there is significantly greater awareness and understanding of ASD today compared to when I was a child in a rural community, I believe there is still much more work to do on a broader scale. I believe I've been relatively fortunate in my life and hope to see other autistic individuals have similar or even better outcomes. I want people to understand that I generally accept and like the way I've grown, despite (or because of) the struggles. I recognize that some individuals are more profoundly affected by autism and may understandably have a much more negative opinion of their diagnosis than I do. I wish for all of us to receive the support, understanding, empowerment, and fulfillment that we rightfully deserve. I also want others to understand that the struggles autistic people face are similar to struggles most, if not all, people face. Help, understanding, and justice cannot be selectively distributed to some while excluding others. They cannot be offered to one race and denied to another, provided to one gender but not to another, or given to straight individuals while neglecting those who identify as LGBTQ+. Ethical and equitable treatment must be extended to everyone, as its absence ultimately diminishes the rights and well-being of all. The support I've had throughout my life is not something everyone on the spectrum has meaningful access to. In fact, I've been told I'm quite fortunate. In many ways that's true, but I often add that circumstances similar to mine should not be a matter of luck. I believe much of that can and should change, but maybe I'm one of those that's passionate to the optimist and naive to the pessimist.

I aspire to continue my journey of exploration and pursuing the things that captivate and inspire me, as I have always done. My hope is to keep gaining a clearer understanding of my purpose and align my actions accordingly. I wish the same for others so they may also experience the happiness and justice I have experienced. My desire is for freedom, justice, inner peace, and fulfillment to be present for all. I long for those who experience these can be inspiring role models for others. Those who accomplish this, particularly within the autism spectrum community, are the individuals I consider to embody not only these virtues but also the essence of true heroism. I feel pride and satisfaction in being part of such a community.

Find out more Joe Shipman here:

Book by Brigitte and Joseph Shipman "A Mother's Guide Through Autism, Through The Eyes of The Guided"

STORY 31:
Tessa Watkins

Autistic Adult, Parent, Programmer, Self-Advocate
Favorite Superhero: Scarlet Witch

I believe a superhero is someone who does the impossible for the good of someone else. In Guardians of the Galaxy, the minimally verbal hero named Groot made the ultimate sacrifice to save their allies. Hodor, a minimally speaking character who traveled with Bran, made the same sacrifice in Game of Thrones. I am autistic but don't count myself among the heroes, let alone the superheroes. I like to think I do good things for others, sure, but the things that I do wouldn't—nay, shouldn't—be considered impossible just because I'm autistic. If I'm doing something that most other humans on this planet can do, then I don't see how the act can be categorized as impossible. However, I can understand and appreciate overcoming a particular challenge that someone said I would never be able to overcome. In that context, someone made a judgment about my abilities and suggested that something was impossible for me, so in their eyes, I did do something impossible by proving them wrong. But then we get into the weeds of objective heroism vs. subjective. I suppose it's very autistic of me to lead my chapter with this analysis;

I needed to process why I would be featured in a book with this title. Objectively, I am not a superhero, but subjectively… perhaps, I am.

From my perspective, my childhood and young adult life were dull. Not boring, just dull. If I experienced emotional or physical pain, it was quickly hidden, pushed down, and away where people couldn't see. In my formative years, I was bothered by a lot of things like noise, texture, and temperature. I was also clumsy and often got small injuries. It would annoy the adults taking care of me, so they eventually turned to ignoring my cries for the small things, or for things they couldn't see wrong that only I felt. By being ignored, I learned that I couldn't trust anyone to help me when I needed it and that I was bothersome for reaching out and trying to communicate my need for help, so I stopped. Unfortunately, a side effect of stopping the pain is stopping the joy. If you let even one ounce of emotion slip out, it might come pouring out like a leaky faucet. For this coping mechanism to be effective, it needs to block all.

I grew up with a single mother, an absent father, and a half-sister who went to her dad's place for the summers. For most of my childhood, we were a family of three living in poverty. Our mother had undiagnosed bipolar disorder and major depression. When asked, she said she knew something was up since she was 18 years old, but she didn't have the resources to seek help until she was almost 40 years old and I was 16. When she finally did get help, they diagnosed her with bipolar type 2, rapid cycling. This diagnosis meant that when I was a kid, my mother was 'emotionally unstable.' She'd quickly cycle between hypomanic and depressive cycles or the full emotional gamut.

I have great memories of her hypomanic episodes, like the time we went to Splash Lagoon, just the two of us, and we ended up napping on the lounge chairs because existing is exhausting. I have awful memories too, like when she couldn't find a specific, important document and forced me and my sister to join in the search for it. I remember crying at the bookshelf, repeatedly leafing through the same pile of papers because I was too scared to move. I didn't know what piece of furniture would go flying next, and I didn't want to get accidentally crushed by getting in her way.

Now, as you read this, keep in mind that I love my mom. She is not the villain in my story. I am diagnosed with complex post-traumatic stress disorder, or CPTSD, caused by ongoing child abuse. Was my mom an abuser? Yes, but not like how you might be thinking. She didn't want to hurt me. She didn't know she was hurting me. My mother loves me, and she did the best she could with the resources she had. So how is it that a loving mother can accidentally abuse their autistic child to the point of giving them CPTSD? Well, just as my PTSD is complex, so is the answer. For starters, it wasn't just my mom.

When they say, "hurt people hurt people," I apply that to my mom, my family, and the people who surrounded me as a child. I could write a whole book alone about my mother and her father on their own undiagnosed (and unmanaged) CPTSD. Child abuse was passed down in my family like an heirloom, except nobody wanted it and nobody had the resources to get rid of it. Rage or ignoring was the coping mechanism most employed when they were overwhelmed and stressed out (and as a kid, you hoped for ignoring). It makes complete sense as to why they did what they did, despite not wanting to do it. It doesn't absolve them of the harm they caused, nor does it make them automatically forgiven, but it does make it make sense.

I remember going to the food bank with my mother as a fond memory. We'd get in line and each of us was given a cardboard box. We'd move through the rooms of this strange building (it seemed like a shed, but bigger) and older people, mostly women, worked like robots on a conveyor belt, putting canned food in our boxes. We'd get to the pastry section, and it was always bread past its sell-by date. If there was mold on it, you'd just cut it off at home. The last section was desserts. Mom always let me choose dessert!

When I was 7 years old, Wednesdays were the best day of the week. My mother wore an ankle bracelet, so it was the only day we got to leave the house to go to the laundromat. My sister and I were disruptive there; we treated it like a playground. We would race around in the laundry carts. I remember her pushing me in one and letting go. We always got yelled at for the ruckus, but it was worth it. 10 out of 10, would do it again.

Now, if you're still trying to justify my mom as a villain because she did time, you still don't know the full story. You don't know what her crime was or who it was against. All you know is that it was unlawful, and she got caught. How many of you would kill to save your children? I'm autistic, so I mean that literally.

The abuse I suffered might be considered as 'just parenting' to families without support or resources, especially if physical assault and/ or emotional manipulation are the only methods of discipline they know how to use. If surviving childhood is what it takes to be a superhero, then all autistic people who make it to adulthood are superheroes, including me.

Find out more about Tessa Watkins here:

https://tessawatkins.com/
https://just1voice.com/
https://aurisecreative.com/

STORY 32:
Greg Zorbas

Autistic Adult, Advocate
Favorite Superhero: Rick Sanchez from Rick and Morty

Individuals with autism interact with the world around them differently than those without autism. Many people are aware that autism comes with some degree of social challenges and differentness, but it can also be a source of creativity and novelty. Since my diagnosis, I've spent time learning about myself and others, and believe that everyone would benefit from having a greater understanding of neurodiversity. Different-ness is actually a good thing for society.

Receiving an autism diagnosis was one of the most pivotal events in my life. I was diagnosed with autism spectrum disorder (ASD) about three years before the writing of this story. Prior to my diagnosis, I thought that one could immediately recognize that someone was autistic just by being in their presence for a short while. Growing up, I didn't personally know any autistic kids and assumed that autistic children went to special schools (not mine). As I found out later in life, one of my autistic skills is sorting. When I was young, without realizing it, I sorted autistic and mental challenges into a 'them' bucket.

The signs of autism were present in my life from the beginning. I had trouble sleeping as a baby, and my parents would spend hours trying to rock me to sleep. As a young child, I had the uniquely autistic habit of banging my head against the pillow for hours while trying to fall asleep. I started taking Tylenol PM in high school, yet I would fail to sleep some nights. As an adult, my sleeping challenges have persisted, despite medications and various meditation methods. Lack of sleep, my low 'social battery' and ADHD can frequently cause me to be irritable and inattentive, something those close to me can readily attest to. I am generally well-intentioned but occasionally come across as cold and callous.

In addition to sleep difficulties, I also had a variety of behavior and attention issues. I pulled other kids' hair in kindergarten. My dad made me read apology letters to my class in grade school for my frequent infractions. I had a rebellious streak in high school and was frequently disruptive in class. My pediatrician and various therapists all failed to consider autism. In high school, I was told by a specialist that I was "too high functioning" for ADHD or any other diagnosis, like many individuals who are diagnosed later in life. In hindsight, I demonstrated every one of the core symptoms of ASD. It is estimated that roughly 1 in 45 people in the United States have autism, yet many people, me included, don't find out until well into adulthood.

Another key feature of my autistic experience has been not 'knowing the rules' for different types of social interactions, especially when experiencing them for the first time. From grade school, I consistently felt like an outsider when moving to a new school, switching sports teams, or joining new friend groups. I switched all these every few years throughout my childhood, so I became accustomed to starting over, and fitting in was often a humbling process. I was never particularly talkative, and up until adulthood,

I always let others introduce themselves first. Without being aware of it, I developed a habit of watching others and noting how they interacted. That would form the template of how I needed to behave. I would always start out ignorant, but through experience and pattern recognition I learned to adapt.

Intersecting with my social struggles was my lack of empathy growing up. I struggled with forming deep bonds with people throughout childhood. I learned etiquette - the rules of society - but never really had an appreciation of other people's subjective experiences. Up until college, I believed that my experience was also everyone else's experience - everyone saw what I saw and drew the same conclusions. This gave me great conviction in arguments but hindered learning new ideas from others. As a result of this, I had challenges appropriately calibrating written communications, both socially and professionally. The words I wrote in an email often were incongruous with the meaning I was trying to convey, which impacted my relationship with supervisors and friends alike. While Elon Musk is often criticized for the randomness and perceived carelessness of his tweets, I strongly relate to 'communication misfires' and having to subsequently explain my actual intent, in its context.

Looking back, it's easy to see how these and other symptoms gave me challenges in everyday areas of life. I got into trouble in school, had a hard time forming new and maintaining friendships, struggled in certain (boring) academic environments, and had difficulties in my career. Receiving the autism diagnosis profoundly improved my understanding of self and changed the course of my personal and professional development.

It's hard to overstate how life-changing it was receiving my diagnosis. It's as if my previous concept of self arose from quick glimpses at disjointed parts of the whole. After my diagnosis, I was able to see my full self, every one of my experiences now had context. All the issues I had experienced growing up such as extreme sensitivity to sound, abrupt or awkward interactions, sleep, and attention issues, being argumentative and defiant, narrow, and deep interests, rigid behavior patterns, and fixed daily routines, were all related to the same underlying cause. I realized that I was no longer a mal-adapted person. I was now an autistic person with my own unique set of experiences. I became invigorated and encouraged rather than trying to subconsciously avoid or bury past issues. I could now systematically approach addressing them. I shed shame and moved into self-reflection and problem-solving.

Taking inventory of my challenges has enabled me to hone focused skills and techniques so that symptoms have turned into strengths (superpowers!). Attention and practice help me to focus on them. Pattern recognition is one of those strengths with broad application. Due to my social discomfort and reliance on observation, I became adept at judging body language. I can size people up quickly and can often detect candor by noticing facial details. Having a built-in BS detector helps me in my career and socially (but very rarely at the poker table). Being mindful of my communication challenges has led to more successful communication approaches. Knowing I'm not the most comfortable with small talk now just means I need conversation topics prepared ahead of time. Mapping out personal and professional conversations (being prepared) has been one of my most significant functional adaptations. Knowing that I'm susceptible to being misunderstood in written communications, I implemented four simple steps to reduce misfires (and the cognitive load used to process these communications):

1. Never send an important email without re-reading it.

2. Always allow several hours to pass before sending a note on an emotionally charged topic. Avoid 'shooting from the hip.'

3. When in doubt, have someone proofread my email or text. My wife, Jess, has been my single most impactful guide in professional communication. I often jokingly ask, "What would a person say here?" The practice has made me significantly more effective in this arena.

4. Use email templates. For example, greeting —> acknowledge context —> present information —> action or request —> gratitude.

Learning empathy through social pattern recognition has been another key skill I've acquired as an adult. Having experienced loss and hardship at various points throughout my life, I'm able to understand the feeling others have when those events are impacting them (sympathy). Using that as a reference, I can empathize with people by relating their current experiences to situations I've experienced in the past. This allows me to sort most of others' experiences into categories, enabling me to connect with people even if I don't know exactly what they're going through (empathy). Earlier in life, I was oblivious to others' needs. Now, I actively apply empathy and generally try to support people.

Additionally, because I understand new concepts by relating them to others I've already experienced, I am constantly sorting and making comparisons to learn. This sorting and pattern recognition process has helped me develop a 'systems perspective,' enabling me to think about problems creatively. Thinking about problems in a multi-factorial way helps me to develop more targeted, effective solutions. Systems thought is one of my superpowers and is very helpful in working across teams or in matrixed organizations where I need to analyze multiple inputs and outputs for a project.

There are a lot of ways I'm continuing to learn and develop, and there are still several obstacles and frustrations I face regularly. Talking openly about mental health challenges has led me to embark on my own journey of self-discovery and has changed the trajectory of my life. The fact that I was so ignorant about my own state of being suggests to me that I have even more to learn about people. Appreciating the complexity of my own situation and experiences has given me a profound appreciation for others around me. In today's chaotic world where opinions and information flow faster than ever, appreciating variety in people and how these differences in experience contribute to our world will be the only way that society can meaningfully progress.

Find out more about Greg Zorbas here:

gregzorbas11@gmail.com

STORY 33:
Rebecca Hale – Concluding Story fromPhysical Therapist

Mom, Advocate, Pediatric Physical Therapist
Favorite Superhero: Wonder Woman

Every individual has a unique human blueprint to offer the world, and each is inherently worthy, contributing a puzzle piece of the overall human experience. That puzzle is full of synchronicities that tie us all together. This is no difference for people with autism. Everyone should be given the opportunity to find and express their unique personalities, gifts, and identities.

Autism is a medical label that often comes with a negative connotation and an idea that behaviors must be tolerated and accommodated. We should shift our perspective away from the notion that behaviors need to be altered and suppressed. Instead, let's understand that we are all, in similar ways, expressing what our nervous systems require.

Let's view the strategies of individuals with autism through the lens of superhero traits. Superheroes are defined by their unique capabilities, uniqueness, and oddities. They have characteristics that we identify as extraordinary or different from the norm. Their uniqueness enhances who they are and how they navigate the world. Generally, it is one hyper-focused trait or strategy that makes that superhero memorable. We honor and celebrate their focused gift. When we look at some of the strategies typically characterized in autism, we can see how these perceived negative behaviors are in fact their bodies' brilliant ways of keeping them safe. When people feel safe, they are able to express their unique talents and gifts optimally.

Here are some superhuman strategies that our nervous system uses to protect ourselves from actual or perceived threats or danger:

ENHANCED SENSES

When Spiderman was bitten by a spider, he acquired the enhanced senses of a spider providing him with an increased overall awareness. Children with autism are often acutely aware of sounds, smells, tastes, and physical sensations creating a highly specific awareness of their environment that filters out information that is not needed to keep them safe. Paying attention to a person's reactions or resistance to different environmental stimuli such as body temperature, tactical pressure, and loud noises can help us learn to decipher their needs and dislikes.

POWER POSING

Picture Wonder Woman, hands on hips, chin up, feet shoulder-width apart, chest popped out. Power posing, a concept coined by Neuroscientist Amy Cuddy, is taking on postures that give the body physiological feedback that the body is safe. Assuming this position, your body will send a message to your brain that you are strong, safe, and able. This shows us that positioning our body can have a physiological impact on our brain's perception of our safety. Similarly, the flapping, jumping, and rocking of children with autism gives their brain feedback that they are moving and seeking safety.

STIMMING

Stimming is the repetition of physical movements, sounds, words, and moving objects and is a natural behavior for self-regulation. There is a misconception that a child who stims is expelling excess energy. In fact, stimming is a response to the nervous system needing to rev up and satisfy the perceived needs of the body. This response will be heightened if they have an expectation or inherent understanding that they need to sit still. Dash from The Incredibles was portrayed as having restless energy. However, his need to acknowledge that the call of his nervous system led to his power of superspeed. Stimming is a physiological response common to many people, click a pen, tap their foot, pick, scratch, and bite their nails. Some behaviors are more 'socially accepted' but they are all performed automatically and for the purpose of keeping the body safe. There are forms of stimming that can be harmful and self-destructive such as hitting or yelling. In these circumstances, it is important to discover and acknowledge what the body needs and find other activities that may satisfy those physiological needs.

HYPERFOCUS

Hyper-focus is a fixation on one thought pattern at a time, to the exclusion of everything else. On a quest, superheroes tend to focus their greatest strength on utilizing their gift to help others. People with autism can be highly productive in the subject they enjoy. They tend to become experts down to the minutia of details. Many things people hyper-focus on as children provide transferable interests later in life. They can have a greater ability to process information about that subject. Research shows us that people with autism have an increased capacity for extended focus on a preferred or obsessive interest. The intensity can be channeled into a willingness to work on difficult tasks. Though often negatively perceived, a narrow scope of learning interest can lead to deep understanding.

Temple Grandin, a superhero in the world of autism, states, "Obsessions, in fact, can be great motivators. A creative teacher or parent can channel obsessions into career-relevant skills."

Here are some great tools for working with children with autism:

TAKE AN INVENTORY

Take an inventory to identify individual stressors. What makes the proverbial cup of tolerance overflow? Journaling for a week can reveal what stressors (environment, people, demands, food, schedules, activities) cause a person with autism to go into a protective mode or explosive response. When that happens, they cannot access their environment and strengths. Demands will only exacerbate the situation.

CREATE A SAFE PREDICTABLE SPACE

Make environmental changes to decrease stressors. Create a 'safe' external environment. Establish a predictable routine. Create safety within expectations and familiarity. Check your own nervous system. Your regulated or dysregulated nervous system will directly impact another's ability to feel safe.

BODY AWARENESS

Use movement to help understand the body in space. Develop the ability to create a safe internal environment. Movement is a gateway to learning. It is through movement exploration that we develop the concepts of positional terms, body control, spatial awareness, retrieval of information from the environment, and promoting brain-body connections. Help find more acceptable strategies as alternatives to excessive movement, flapping, mouthing, scratching, audible noises, and the like. Learn through guided, facilitated movement. Use tactile pressure to help feel your body in space. Allow the body to get what it needs through movement.

TEACHING INTEROCEPTION (the ability to sense and discern signals from the body)

Help the person notice and identify sensations that show that their nervous system needs something. Awareness of the sensations is the first step which leads to the ability to recognize their behaviors are a result of unmet needs. Identify needs and what can be done to address them. It will be helpful for them to understand how these needs emanate from the nervous system and how these needs can be satisfied. This will help them begin to figure out how to regulate their internal environment despite the external environment.

CLOSING

People with autism bravely highlight for the rest of us how challenging the human experience can be navigating environments, personalities, and demands of this sensory-saturated world. If we are truly honest with ourselves, many of us demonstrate compensatory strategies and addictive behaviors that help us tolerate, survive, and hopefully thrive. Our nervous system responds subconsciously to how we respond at any given moment to the experiences we have as we journey through life.

These stories highlight the many human experiences that people with autism have when striving for a fulfilling human experience. Not only can we empathize but often threads of the stories can be so relatable and can lead us to learn a whole lot about ourselves and our behaviors. It can make us consider how this world challenges us and how we often dampen or suppress difficult experiences with our own coping mechanisms. The nervous system brilliantly highlights when the environment is making our cup overflow.

We can empower students, teachers, and parents to listen to the body's messages through movement and provide them with tools and language for learning and self-regulation while making adjustments and having consideration for individual human needs.

Visit my website for resources and videos related to the tools for regulating the nervous system.

Find out more about Rebecca Hale here:

www.turtlehouz.com

CONCLUSION

As we arrive at the end of this volume of "Superheroes on the Spectrum," we find ourselves immersed in a world rich with awareness, acceptance, and celebration of neurodiversity. The voices within this book have woven a tapestry of experiences, thoughts, and emotions that span continents, generations, and perspectives. What we've discovered along the way is a testament to the resilience and extraordinary nature of individuals on the autism spectrum.

Our journey began with a philosophy deeply rooted in the belief that understanding, embracing, and celebrating neurodiversity enriches us all. We embarked on this path guided by a steadfast commitment to showing real life with autism, both the challenges, and the gifts it bestows. We recognize that just as autism is a spectrum, our contributors represent an equally diverse spectrum of voices. We've shown the diverse experiences of people on the autism spectrum, from adults facing life's challenges to the "voices" of non-verbal children. We've also highlighted the vital role of parents, caregivers, family members and community, giving you a real picture of life on the spectrum.

Our contributors hail from different corners of the world—the United States, the United Kingdom, and South Africa. They bring with them vastly different perspectives on symbols, language, causes, and treatment. We've been honored to include the voices of non-speaking autistic adults and children, and we've celebrated the enduring dedication of moms and dads who tirelessly advocate for their loved ones. The diversity of our contributors and the unique richness of their perspectives stand as a testament to the central tenets of our philosophy: awareness, acceptance, and celebration of all things related to autism.

In our quest to honor the invaluable contributions of our contributors, we've preserved the diverse language they use when discussing diagnosis, severity levels, functioning, and identity. The symbols that adorn our cover—the puzzle piece, the color spectrum, and the infinity symbol—mirror the myriad symbols that resonate with the individuals we've featured within these pages. These symbols, like our book, are bridges that connect us to a deeper understanding of the autism experience. Our intention has never been to make everyone happy, but rather to embrace the multifaceted perspectives that exist today, all while keeping our focus unwaveringly on awareness, acceptance, and the celebration of strengths.

As we wrap up this volume, let us reflect on the broader significance of what we've uncovered. In a world that often amplifies differences and promotes conformity, "Superheroes on the Spectrum" reminds us that diversity is a source of strength, beauty, and resilience. Autism, in all its intricacies, embodies this very essence of diversity. It's a spectrum where each individual is a unique expression of human potential, with their own set of challenges and, more importantly, their own extraordinary gifts.

Our contributors have eloquently shared their stories of triumph and tribulation, of moments filled with frustration and those bursting with joy. Through their narratives, they've unveiled a world where daily interactions can be laced with the nuances of sensory sensitivities, where communication is as diverse as the colors in a rainbow, and where the journey towards self-acceptance is both deeply personal and profoundly universal.

As we close this chapter, we must acknowledge the pervasive judgment and criticism that many of us, both within and outside the autism community, have faced in our lives. The world has not always understood the richness that neurodiversity brings to our collective human experience. But within these pages, we've created a sanctuary—a space where acceptance and understanding reign supreme. We've cast aside the weight of judgment and criticism, replacing it with the lightness of empathy and appreciation.

In the embrace of our diverse narratives, we find unity. In our openness to different symbols, languages, and perspectives, we discover the true meaning of inclusion. And in our relentless pursuit of awareness, acceptance, and the celebration of strengths, we uncover the superpowers that lie within each of us.

To those who live on the spectrum, we celebrate you as the superheroes you are. Your unique abilities, your resilience, and your unwavering spirit inspire us all. You are the embodiment of courage, the champions of understanding, and the architects of a world where diversity is not just tolerated but cherished.

To the parents and caregivers who walk this path alongside their loved ones, your dedication and unwavering support are the wind beneath the capes of these superheroes. You are the pillars of strength that make every achievement possible, and your love knows no bounds.

To our readers, whether you are on the spectrum or not, we invite you to join us in this celebration of diversity. Our hope is that these stories will not only raise awareness but also ignite a spark of acceptance and celebration within your hearts. In the spirit of embracing neurodiversity, we encourage you to take this newfound understanding out into the world, to be advocates for inclusion and high-quality equitable care, and to recognize the superpowers that reside within us all.

Thank you for joining us on this remarkable journey, and may the spirit of awareness, acceptance, and celebration continue to shine brightly in your hearts and in the world around you.

With boundless gratitude and a profound sense of possibility,

Jeannette and Crystal

RELATED RESOURCES AND LINKS

We're also very excited to donate a portion of the proceeds from sales of this book to the following two non-profit organizations:

- **KFM Making A Difference** is an organization focused on spreading disability awareness and giving scholarships for students with autism to pursue a post-secondary education. Founded in 2009 by CEO and President Kerry Magro, the organization hopes to "make a difference" in the lives of all of those with special needs.

- **American Autism & Rehabilitation Foundation (AARF)** is an organization that provides therapeutic services, events, and support to the lives of children, adults, and families affected by various special needs conditions. AARF is dedicated to serving families, children, and adults with all types of neurological conditions such as Autism, Asperger's Syndrome, Cerebral Palsy, Down Syndrome, ADD/ADHD, sensory processing disorder, and more.

Numerous resources and links were cited throughout the stories and are listed here for reference.

Rev. Jeannette Paxia www.innersuperhero.org
www.innersuperhero.me
Instagram: your_inner_superhero
TikTok: inner_superhero
App - Inner Superhero
Podcast: Ordinary People Extraordinary
Lives hosted on Word Of Mom Radio

Dr. Crystal Morrison www.meerkatvillage.com
www.thevillagevision.com
LinkedIn: https://www.linkedin.com/in/
drcrystalmorrison/
Podcast: The Village Vision podcast hosted on Word Of Mom Radio

Karye Brockert LinkedIn: https://www.linkedin.com/in/
karye-brockert/

Kelly Cain www.autismcaringcenter.com
https://www.linkedin.com/in/
kelly-cain-73b43a14b/

Carrie Cariello www.carriecariello.com
Facebook: Carrie Cariello
Carrie is the Amazon Best Selling author of "What Color Is Monday, How Autism Changed One Family for the Better," "Someone I'm With Has Autism," and her latest book, "Half My Sky, Autism, Marriage, and the Messiness that is Building a Family"

Angela Chapes	LinkedIn: https://www.linkedin.com/in/angela-chapes-ba062564/
Nicky Cuesta	www.buildingleadershipmindset.com https://link.creedpro.co/widget/bookings/virtualcoffee30
Nicole DeWard	www.shinehw.com www.rise-coffeetea.com LinkedIn: https://www.linkedin.com/in/nicoledeward/
Liz Gabor	www.LizGabor.com
Dr. Daniel Gary	LinkedIn: https://www.linkedin.com/in/daniel-gary-773aaa180/
Dr. Emile Gouws	LinkedIn: https://www.linkedin.com/in/emile-gouws-610449116/
Maximus Jarl	LinkedIn: https://www.linkedin.com/in/maximus-jarl-04b318215 Facebook: facebook.com/max.jarl.73 Instagram: instagram.com/maxjarl
Courtney Kaplan	www.transplanthope.com LinkedIn: www.linkedin.com/in/courtney-kaplan-b59027bb Facebook: facebook.com/courtney.kaplan.52/ Instagram: instagram.com/courtneybkaplan/

Gina Kavali	YouTube and Facebook: Life with the Spectrum Gkasts.com LinkedIn: https://www.linkedin.com/in/gina-kavali-44550813/
Lyric Gillenwaters	YouTube: LyricalGamester
Becky Large	Champion Autism Network: https://championautismnetwork.com/ Autism Travel Club: https://autismtravel.club/
Bobby Latherton	His book *My World, In My Words* is available at Waterstones in Middlesbrough, North Yorkshire (UK) or online at Amazon.
Dr. Kerry Magro	https://kfmmakingadifference.org/ Facebook: Kerry's Autism Journey Kerry is the author of several best-selling books including "Defining Autism From The Heart," "Autism and Falling in Love," "I Will Light It Up Blue," and "Autistics on Autism."
Nicholas McMahill	Facebook: Nicholas's Journey
Caryn Mittleman	Website: ItIsAllGood.org
Jamiel Owens	Facebook: The Ausome Show and Ausomeness Inc. Instagram: @theausomeshow and @ausomenessinc Linkedin: https://www.linkedin.com/in/jamiel-owens-75a985213/

Nicole Pasker	B2hopecoaching@gmail.com
Donna Richards	https://autismfamilycircus.com/
Maria Alejandra Rincón	Instagram: @mariaarincon_tcb
Vincent Rinicella	https://theunfilteredmindofvincent.wordpress.com/
Jeremy Rochford	www.OurNeuroFam.com
Heidi Rome	You Just Have to Love Me: Mothering Instructions From My Autistic Child https://www.momsspectrumoasis.com/ LinkedIn: https://www.linkedin.com/in/heidi-rome-8b60a110/
Richard Schreiber	https://www.linkedin.com/in/richardschreiber/ https://autisminnovationcommunityfoundation.org/ - events targeted to parents and caregivers of autistic members to provide access to more holistic, innovative and tech-oriented autism supports. Host of NYC Autism Tech, Innovation and Careers expo in New York City.
Brigitte Shipman and Joe Shipman	https://www.mothersguidethroughautism.com/ Book by Brigitte and Joseph Shipman "A Mother's Guide Through Autism, Through The Eyes of The Guided"

Tessa Watkins	https://tessawatkins.com/
	https://just1voice.com/
	https://aurisecreative.com/
Greg Zorbas	gregzorbas11@gmail.com
Rebecca Hale	www.turtlehouz.com

ABOUT THE AUTHORS

Rev. Jeannette Paxia

Rev. Paxia is a 2-time #1 International Bestselling Author, sought-after speaker, and coach for adults and children. She's passionate about helping adults and children live the life that they want to live, no matter what age they are. Jeannette achieves her goals through one-on-one coaching, group coaching, speaking, and writing. Along with her business partners, Barbara Alvarado and Gary LaHue, she enjoys sharing wellness activities in the community with their non-profit The Dragonfly Art and Wellness Center.

In her 'spare' time, Jeannette enjoys spending time with her husband and children, walking her dogs, gardening, spending time in nature, and reading.

Dr. Crystal Morrison

Dr. Morrison is a highly regarded executive advisor, strategist, leader, scientist, and tech entrepreneur. While progressing in her career as a scientist, Dr. Morrison was also growing her family. She has three amazing children and has spent almost 20 years navigating the complex system of care and advocating for her children. Her experience inspired her to co-found Meerkat Village, a software company dedicated to improving outcomes for children with special needs by building collaboration and communication among adults providing care. On her journey, she's met countless people working at the intersection of community, education, health care and mental health. She created an exciting new podcast called The Village Vision to celebrate their stories and ignite action.

In her 'spare' time, Crystal enjoys reading, house projects with her husband, annoying her children and snuggling with her dog.

More Books From

   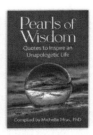

   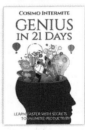 

  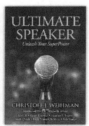  

www.PerfectPublishing.com

More Books From  PERFECT PUBLISHING

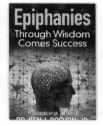

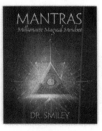
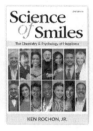

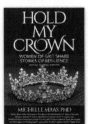

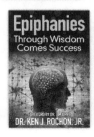

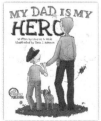

www.PerfectPublishing.com

Made in the USA
Las Vegas, NV
30 November 2023

81870876R00122